SUPER-GAMES

Hutchinson & Co. (Publishers) Ltd

An imprint of the Hutchinson Publishing Group

17–21 Conway Street, London W1P 6JD

Hutchinson Publishing Group (Australia) Pty Ltd
PO Box 496, 16–22 Church Street, Hawthorne, Melbourne,
Victoria 3122
PO Box 151, Broadway, New South Wales 2007

Hutchinson Group (NZ) Ltd
32–34 View Road, PO Box 40–086, Glenfield, Auckland 10

Hutchinson Group (SA) Pty Ltd
PO Box 337, Bergvlei 2012, South Africa

First published 1984
Text and illustrations © Ivan Moscovich 1984

Set in Monophoto Rockwell Light and printed in
Great Britain by Jolly & Barber Ltd, Rugby, Warwickshire
Bound by Anchor Brendon Ltd, Tiptree, Essex

British Library Cataloguing in Publication Data

Moscovich, Ivan
    Ivan Moscovich's super-games.
    1. Puzzles
    I. Title
    793.73   GV1493

ISBN 0 09 156381 X

Ivan Moscovich's SUPER-GAMES

IVAN MOSCOVICH

consultant editor
IAN STEWART

HUTCHINSON

LONDON MELBOURNE SYDNEY AUCKLAND JOHANNESBURG

4 Contents

I have been designing and inventing puzzles, games and toys for the last thirty years or so. During that period I also conceived and created a science museum with a planetarium – among other things. Today I devote all my time to the creation of games and toys – and I enjoy every moment of it.

Many of the games and puzzles in this book are completely original; others are novel adaptations of more traditional games. I hope that the book will convey to the reader my enthusiasm for and fascination with games, and my approach to their creation and design. It combines entertainment with an intellectual challenge, through which a great number of concepts, basic to art, science and mathematics, may be tackled.

It is an open-ended book; there are many opportunities for the reader to modify games in his or her own way, and to invent new variations. I hope that this will cause a chain reaction: the reader will play the games, try to solve the problems, and be stimulated to create his own rules and designs, his own games, puzzles and aesthetic structures. I believe that the topics included open up wide areas of new territory for the inventor of games.

Despite the diversity of topics, there is an underlying continuity: an interplay between geometry and combinatorics (the different ways objects can be arranged). The arrangement of the book will enable the reader to pick out individual topics from this integrated whole. The games and puzzles included are designed so that they can easily be made by the average enthusiast. They do not need special skills or materials, mostly card and paint. Colour is important, and the many coloured illustrations depict examples not just of games, but of beautiful designs and patterns which arise out of the games.

These are not just numerically inspired visual patterns. They can excite the mind, suggest new ideas and insights, new modes of thought and creative expression. In fact, the creation of such compositions may become an exciting activity in its own right.

The topics selected are biased towards visual geometrical concepts, with a strong emphasis on structure and pattern, rather than numerical concepts and word games. This bias is, of course, intended. I have always been fascinated by the interaction of geometry and combinatorics, two powerful ideas which can lead to so many surprising discoveries and complexities, all by using a small number of basic elements as building blocks and operating with them according to simple rules.

The book is designed so that each individual item stands by itself (even if it is in fact related to others), so the reader can dip in at will. This should render it 'frustration-free'.

6 Problem-solving & creativity

Problem-solving can teach us a little about the way our brains function. Thinking can be hard work, hence the natural human tendency to do as little of it as possible. This is visible in the hit-and-run approach to problem-solving: pick the first solution that comes to mind and run with it. Our minds become trapped in their own preconceptions. Information that might solve the problem is not so much neglected as simply not perceived.

The process by which we get ideas is called **conceptualization**. What is conceptualization? It is the process by which we get ideas. At bottom, we know little more than this about it. Conceptualization is the key to problem-solving, a source of mental leverage. If our first idea fails to solve the problem, it is better to try another. The greater the choice of creative concepts, the more chance there is of finding an answer.

Conceptual blocks are mental walls. They obscure our perception of the essence of a problem. They blind us to solutions, sometimes simple and ultimately obvious.

There are many ways to build these mental walls. Inadequate clues, misleading information, overattention to the wrong details, too narrow a point of view. Creators of puzzles exploit these to lead our minds up blind alleys.

Conceptual blocks afflict us all. But, despite them, some minds are able to tackle a problem of bewildering complexity, to penetrate to its core, and to extract an insight of startling simplicity and elegance that solves the problem at a stroke.

A good problem is seldom what it seems. Its solution may demand that a familiar object be used in an unfamiliar way, that a conventional assumption be abandoned, that components be assembled in an unusual arrangement. The direct, head-on approach seldom bears fruit; the lengthy detour may in the end prove shorter. Mental walls are for walking round, not for beating one's brains against.

The horse-and-rider problem

Using only your eyes, can you work out how to mount the riders on their horses?

(Solution: page 110)

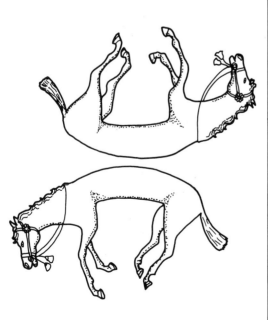

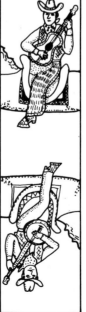

The impossible domino bridge problem

At first sight the structure below is impossible to build. But if you think about it the right way, you can work out how to do it – and even build it yourself

(Solution: page 110)

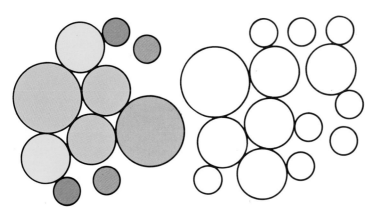

The circles-colouring problem

The figure on the left contains all the logical clues needed to colour the figure on the right

(Solution: page 110)

Insight comes from adopting a novel viewpoint, from thinking sideways, from recentring our attention. What brings it about is still a mystery, the most baffling problem of all.

Insight is a subconscious leap, achieved after a good deal of apparently fruitless conscious thought. But that activity serves to stir the previously placid surface of the subconscious mind into a whirling turmoil of ideas; ideas that shift, bounce, collide and ultimately interlock. . . . Aha! Insight.

Insight is often sudden, seldom unearned.

Two horses, two riders: pair them off. But the pieces will not fit. A mental rearrangement, as well as a physical one, may be needed.

A structure built of dominoes, that would collapse as soon as the first few bricks were laid. . . . But who is to say which bricks must be laid first? Or where the scaffolding may have gone?

A pattern of circles, brightly coloured, concealing a system of rules that must be deduced before they can be applied to another, uncoloured, pattern. Elusive as an undiscovered law of nature.

A trivial jigsaw with four pieces, unworthy of a child of four. Yet the pieces will not fit. How many ways are there to assemble four pieces? More than you imagine. How many can you think of? The one you've omitted is the one you seek. . . .

The quest for insight is as ancient as mankind itself. What we lack is insight about insight itself. To quote Thomas Cottle: 'The history of efforts to understand the creative process, the creative mind, the creative spirit, is long and marvellously filled to the brim with suggestions and theories, anecdotes, vignettes, first-hand reports, and all the signs of real data, hard data and soft data, true data and may be less true data – and still little is understood.'

The classical T puzzle

Copy and cut out the four pieces, and use them to form a perfect capital letter T.
Easy, isn't it?
This is a classic example of how an apparently easy problem can lead to a conceptual block

(Solution: page 110)

8 Lines & linkages

The dimensions of space begin with a point. 'A point,' said Euclid, 'is position without size.' A mathematical abstraction, whose dimensions are zero. The tiniest imaginable portion of space.

The first dimension begins with a line. To build a line, observe the trace of a moving point. A single number suffices to locate any point within the line – its distance from some other, arbitrarily chosen, point. A space whose points can be specified by one number is called **one-dimensional.**

A line is the idealization of a rigid rod. Problems about linked rods are problems in the geometry of lines. Mechanics is a form of geometry. A moving line traces out a plane: a space of two dimensions, requiring two numbers to specify a single point – how far north, how far east.

A **linkage** in the plane is a system of rods, or lines, connected to each other by movable joints, or fixed to the plane by pivots about which they can turn freely. Given a number of rigid rods, can a linkage be found that will produce, by the **motion** of one of its points, a straight line? Pivot a single rod at one end; how does the free end move? In a circle. Circular motion is easy and natural for linkages. The trick is to construct straight-line motion in the absence of a fixed straight line.

This is not just a theoretical problem in geometry. The natural motion produced by a steam engine is rotary. While it can be converted to straight-line motion by a piston, pistons require bearings and bearings are subject to wear. A linkage would provide a more satisfactory solution. The first practical solution, devised by James Watt (1736–1819), the inventor of steam engines, was only approximate. The true curve of motion was an elongated figure 8, a segment of which was close enough to a straight line for Watt's purposes.

From strips of card with holes punched in them and joined by eyelets, you can easily create Watt's Linkage, and many others, and perform experiments.

Watt's Linkage traces a complex mathematical curve known as **Bernoulli's Lemniscate**. It is curious that this is more easily generated by a linkage than is a straight line.

The first mechanical device to produce exact straight-line motion is Peaucellier's Linkage, invented in 1864. It is based on a general geometrical principle called **inversion**. Six links, four of equal length, form an inverter: if a particular point in the linkage follows a curve, then another point follows the inverse curve. The inverse curve to a straight line is a circle. A final, seventh, link constrains one of the points to a circle: the other is forced to follow its inverse, the straight line. By a single general insight, the impossible is converted to the familiar.

A moving plane generates a space of three dimensions, a solid, requiring three numbers to specify any point. By allowing linkages to move out of the plane and into space, a new variety of forms can be created.

How to create a straight line

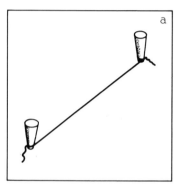
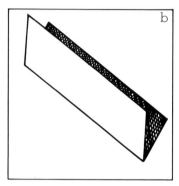

[a] by the ancient rope-stretching method – stretching a thread or rope between two points

[b] by folding a piece of paper

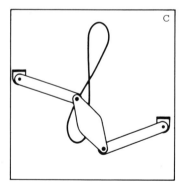
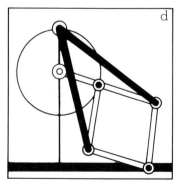

[c] by means of Watt's Linkage

[d] by means of Peaucellier's Linkage

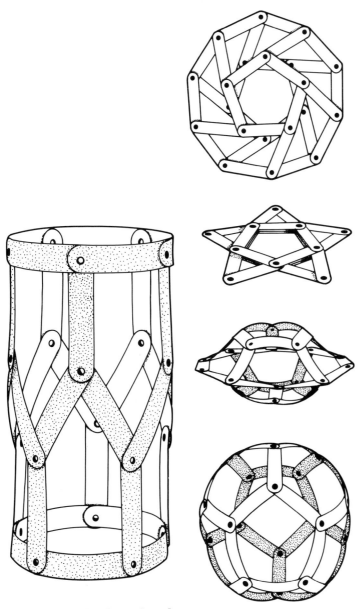

If a number of equal rods are linked in a circle, they form a regular polygon. The ancient Greeks knew that there were only five different solids that could be assembled from identical regular polygons, arranged identically at every junction. These were the **tetrahedron**, with four triangular faces; the **cube**, with six squares; the **octahedron**, with eight triangles; the **dodecahedron**, with twelve pentagons; and the **icosahedron**, with twenty triangles.

All of these can be assembled from enough identical links. Here we see (lower right) a dodecahedron, made from thirty links joined in threes, assembled in rings five at a time. But linkages have the added virtue of flexibility. By moving the links it is possible to create a remarkable variety of forms: a cylinder, a star, a ten-sided polygon (decagon), and an object resembling a flying saucer. Much of the beauty of the original regular solid is retained by these distortions, and the extra lack of regularity and familiarity can arouse our interest. Other geometrical forms can be built from links and subjected to distortions, with equally intriguing results.

Linkage dodecahedron

Many early mechanical moving toys employed linkages in a variety of ingenious ways.
Thirty linkage strips connected by eyelets produce an exciting kinetic structure, which can be transformed into an endless number of plane and three-dimensional forms

10 The great divide

If a plane is cut along a straight line, it divides neatly into two regions. Two cuts can divide each of these regions into two again, giving a total of four regions.

Can a third cut divide all four of these parts in two? If so, there would be eight regions formed by three lines. But in fact there are only seven: the third line can be made to pass through three of the previous four regions, but it cannot encounter all of them. As a result, only seven pieces can be formed by making three cuts.

What is the largest number of regions that can be formed by four straight lines in the plane? Five? Can you guess a general rule for the number of regions formed by **n** lines? Can you prove it?

This problem is one of the simplest in a branch of mathematics called **combinatorial geometry**. There is a fascinating interplay between shapes and numbers. A great many variations on the theme are possible.

For example, what is the largest number of non-overlapping triangles that can be drawn with a given number of straight lines? The largest number of triangles of different sizes? Experiment with the smaller numbers first, then seek a general rule.

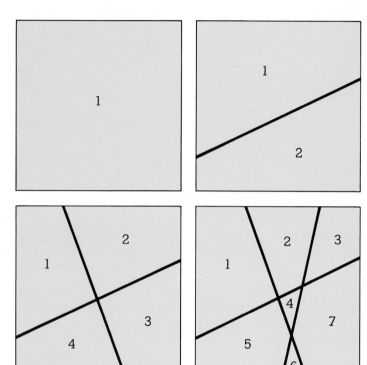

Lines and regions

What is the largest number of regions a plane can be divided into by four, five, six and seven straight lines?

The six-line problem

In the figure six lines enclose eight triangles of three different sizes. Can you find a completely different and simpler way of drawing six straight lines which enclose eight triangles of only two different sizes?

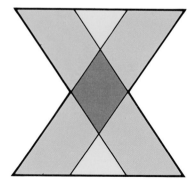

(Solution: page 111)

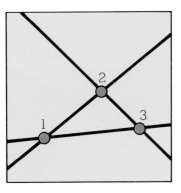 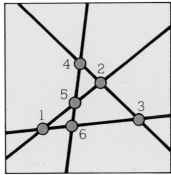

Line intersections

How three or four lines can meet

The seven-line problem

What is the largest number of non-overlapping triangles
that can be produced by drawing seven straight lines?
A six-triangle solution is illustrated. Can you do better?

(Solution: page 111)

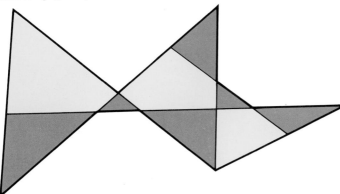

Ten points on five straight lines

Arrange ten points so that
they lie on five lines. Each
line has four points. How
many different kinds of
solution can you find?

(Solution: page 111)

Two straight lines, if not parallel,
must meet in exactly one point, their
intersection. Three lines can meet
in at most three points; four lines in
six.

What is the general answer? In other
words, what is the largest number
of points in which **n** distinct straight
lines can meet?

Experiment using drinking straws
or pencil and paper. Here's a hint: to
get the maximum number of points
each line may be expected to meet
all the others. Can this always be
arranged?

In fact, all that is necessary is for
each line to avoid passing through
the previous intersections, and to
avoid being parallel to any of the
previous lines. Out of the infinitude
of possible lines, only a finite (though
large) number violate these conditions. So it is indeed possible to
make each line meet all the others.
It follows that the **n**th line added
produces a further **n**-1 points. So
the numbers follow this pattern:

LINES	INTERSECTIONS	TOTAL
2	1	1
3	1+2	3
4	1+2+3	6
5	1+2+3+4	10
6	1+2+3+4+5	15
7	1+2+3+4+5+6	21

These are the **triangular numbers**,
known from antiquity. The **n**th triangular number is equal to $\frac{1}{2}n(n-1)$.
Another type of problem with lines
is to produce configurations obeying given restrictions. For example,
arrange a given number of lines to
meet in a given number of points.

Now let's see just how imaginative you are. Draw nine dots on a piece of paper, arranged in a 3 × 3 square. Take your pencil and draw a single line, broken into no more than **four** straight pieces, that will pass through all nine dots. Do not lift your pencil from the paper.

This is a typical example of the type of problem which at first sight appears impossible. Eight dots . . . easy! But nine?

If you can't see how to solve it, you've run head first into a conceptual block, and a typical one: the tendency to take too narrow a view of the problem. Are you assuming that lines must be hori-zontal or vertical? To be sure, that's how the dots naturally arrange themselves . . . but nobody said the lines had to go in **any** particular direction. Diagonals would provide new possibilities.

Then again, although the square of dots has a natural square boundary, nothing in the problem says that your lines have to stay **within** that boundary. Mental walls. . . .

The great value of an insight is that, once gained, it may be generalized. If you can solve the problem of the nine dots, you will have little difficulty solving the apparently more complicated problems of the twelve dots and the sixteen dots.

The nine-point problem

Connect the nine points with four straight lines without lifting your pencil. Can you do it with three lines as well?

(Solution: page 111)

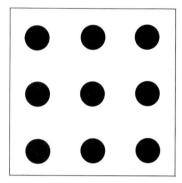

The sixteen-point problem

The sixteen points can be connected by six straight lines, without raising the pencil and without going through any point twice.

There are many solutions (one is shown on page 111). Find one in which the sixteen points are connected by a continuous path formed from six straight-line segments and making a closed loop

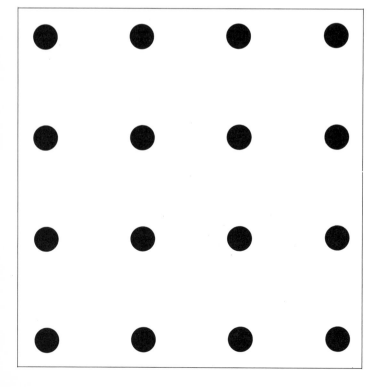

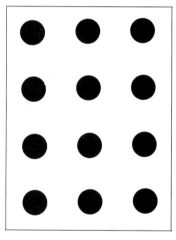

The twelve-point problem

What is the smallest number of line segments needed to produce a continuous broken line (having corners where necessary) through twelve dots?

(Solution: page 111)

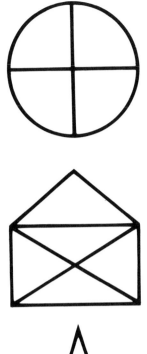

Leonhard Euler was a Swiss mathematician who lived from 1707 to 1783 and wrote more mathematical research than anyone else in history. At that time, the town of Königsberg had seven bridges, and it is said that the people of the town had never been able to solve the problem: is it possible to go for a walk, cross each bridge once only, and return home?

Euler solved the problem by replacing it with something that looked simpler. Given a figure composed of lines joining points, is it possible to traverse the figure in one continuous path, without taking your pencil from the paper and without going over any line twice? Euler showed that there would have to be at the most **two** places where an odd number of lines meet; and if a return to the start is required, there would have to be **no** places where an odd number of lines meet. The reasoning is simple, once seen: a continuous journey will enter each such junction exactly as often as it leaves – except at the start and finish.

The problem of the Königsberg bridges is then solved by noting that it is equivalent to traversing such a network of lines, which has **four** junctions with an odd number of lines. So no solution can exist. Euler's problem is really one of **topology**, a branch of mathematics that deals with properties of figures that are preserved by continuous distortions. Two networks are topologically equivalent if one can be distorted to give the other. If a network can be traversed by a single curve, so can any topologically equivalent network. Another topic arising from Euler's work is **graph theory**, the study of networks formed by lines connecting points.

Not bad for one recreational puzzle!

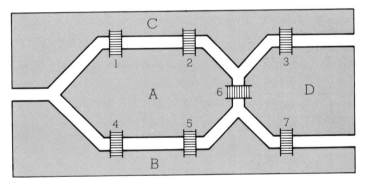

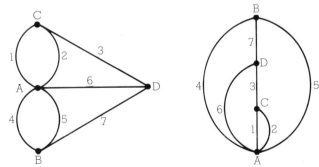

At a stroke

Trace each figure without lifting the pen from the paper, drawing each line once only.
One is impossible: which?

The seven bridges of Königsberg

The top diagram shows the archetypal network-traversing problem. Can the people of Königsberg go for a walk, crossing every bridge exactly once?
Below are two topologically equivalent networks, whose traversal is tantamount to solving the problem

We have talked of points moving in the plane. A **transformation** of the plane is a motion of its points. Among the possible types of transformations, the important ones for geometry are the **rigid motions** or **isometries**, which move figures but do not change their shape or size. (The name is from the Greek: **isos**, the same; **metros**, measure.) There are four basic types of isometry of the plane:

TRANSLATION (slide)

ROTATION (turn)

REFLECTION (mirror image)

GLIDE REFLECTION (slide and reflect)

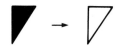

The two triangles are exactly identical. Geometrically, it is said they are **congruent**, meaning that by suitable motion one may be perfectly superimposed on the other. Evidently that motion can be carried out in a plane, i.e. in two dimensions, simply by sliding one triangle on top of the other (translation and rotation).

But what about these two triangles? One is the mirror image of the other. No motion keeping the triangles in the plane will superimpose them. One must be lifted out of the plane into the third dimension, turned over, and replaced in the plane.

Transformations and isometries of plane

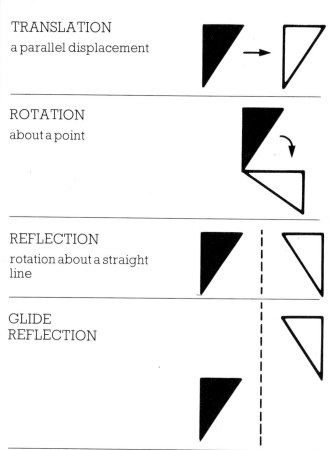

TRANSLATION
a parallel displacement

ROTATION
about a point

REFLECTION
rotation about a straight line

GLIDE REFLECTION

An isometry which changes the sense (clockwise or anticlockwise) is called **opposite**; one which preserves the sense is **direct**. Translations and rotations are direct isometries; reflections and glide reflections are opposite

SYMMETRIES
are those isometries which transform the figure into itself

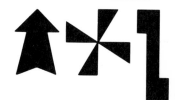

Fitting shapes into holes

It can be seen that an isosceles triangle can fit in two ways into a hole of the identical shape

a scalene triangle in only one way

while an equilateral triangle in six possible positions

In how many different ways can you fit a square into its hole?

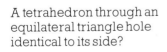 

A tetrahedron through an equilateral triangle hole identical to its side?

A cube through a hole identical to its side?

The ancient geometric theorem attributed to Pythagoras is one of the select few theorems that almost everybody has at least a nodding acquaintance with. It deals with the relationship between the two shorter sides of a right-angled triangle and the longer side (hypotenuse). In words: **the square on the hypotenuse is the sum of the squares on the other two sides.** In symbols,

$$a^2 + b^2 = c^2$$

where a and b are the lengths of the two shorter sides, and c is the length of the hypotenuse. But what does this actually mean? In numerical terms, it means that we may construct right-angled triangles by using any three lengths a, b, c that satisfy the Pythagorean condition

$$a^2 + b^2 = c^2.$$

For example,

$$3^2 + 4^2 = 9 + 16 = 25 = 5^2,$$

so a triangle with sides 3, 4, 5 is necessarily right-angled. There are many whole-number Pythagorean Triples like this, for example, 5, 12, 13 and 8, 15, 17. The general rule for finding all Pythagorean Triples is known, and was one of the first results to be obtained in the theory of Diophantine Equations, that is, equations to be solved with whole numbers. So there is a surprising link between geometry and the theory of numbers.

Geometrically, the Pythagorean Theorem asserts an equality of **areas**. The square whose side is the hypotenuse c has exactly the same area as the two other squares combined. It is an interesting problem to demonstrate this directly, by finding a way to cut up the two smaller squares into pieces which may be assembled to form the larger square. (Solution: page 112) There is an alternative and very beautiful solution to this problem, known as Perigal's Dissection, in which the smallest square remains intact and the middle-sized square is cut into four pieces of the same shape and size.

The Egyptian triangle

The surveyors of ancient Egypt, it is said, used this triangle to construct near perfect right angles. Divide a rope into twelve equal parts by knots. Use it to form a triangle whose sides are in the ratio 3:4:5. (Note $3+4+5=12$.) Then one angle will be a right angle

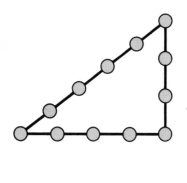

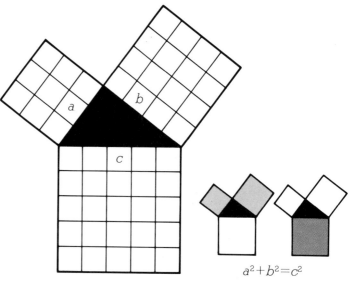

$$a^2+b^2=c^2$$

Pythagorean puzzle

Cut out the six pieces.
On the right-angled triangle
build

[a] a square on the
 hypotenuse using the
 five remaining pieces

[b] a square on the longer
 of the other two sides
 using only the four
 identical pieces

You have now proved the
Pythagorean Theorem, as
well as solved the puzzle

(Solution: page 112)

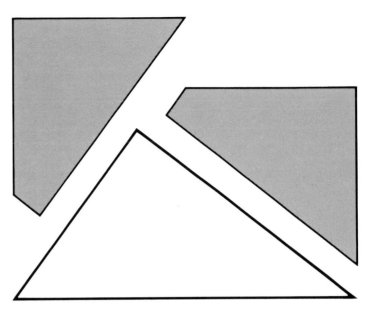

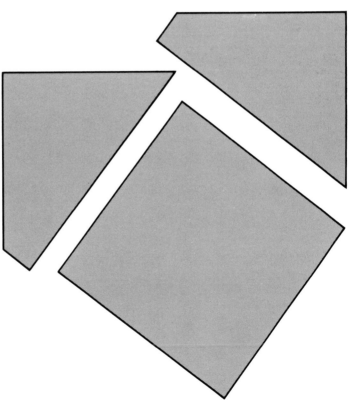

18 Pythagorino

With a little patience, you can create a completely novel and rewarding domino game concept, based on the basic shape of the Pythagorean Theorem.

The illustrations contain all the relevant information to create and colour the game.

It consists of a set of twenty-seven shapes, coloured in three colours, which appear in different combinations on each shape.

The set of twenty-seven pieces is obtained by starting with an isosceles right-angled triangle and constructing squares on its three sides. Such a shape is most easily formed by drawing a square grid, **together with its diagonals**; the Pythagorean configuration may then be assembled by combining some of the resulting small triangles together (see how the shapes overlap such a grid in the lower left illustration).

The game itself may be played on such a grid, or in a free version without a board at all. Players take turns to place their shapes, one at a time. Adjacent shapes must touch either along two big squares or pairs of small squares (lower right). The red player scores a point for each of his big squares that touches another big red square; similarly for violet. Isolated red or violet squares, not touching another, do not count.

The player who has the largest number of points wins. In the event of the scores being equal, the player with the smallest number of connected strips of squares contributing to his score wins.

The game can be played on a square matrix board of 14×14 squares, with all its diagonals, but can be played also without the restriction of a board.

Game sample

A game won by the red player. Six of the big red squares are connected to others, so red scores 6. Similarly, violet scores 6. But red achieves his score with only two connected strips of squares, whereas violet requires three strips; so red wins. Note that disconnected red or violet squares score no points

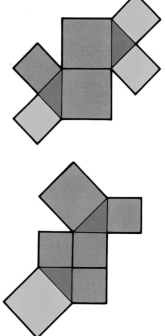

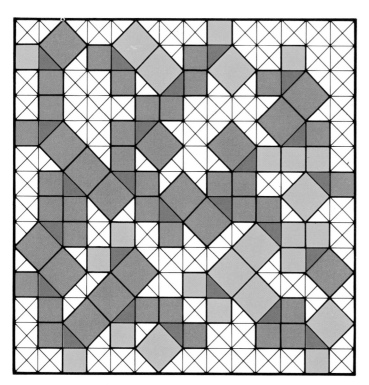

Pythagorino

Two ways to join shapes: the edges must match, with either big or small squares together

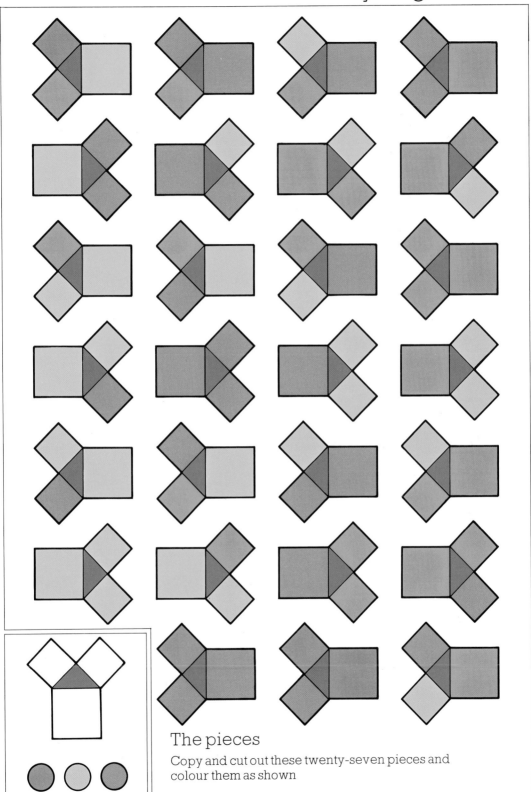

The pieces

Copy and cut out these twenty-seven pieces and colour them as shown

We have already referred, in respect of Euler's work on the problem of the Königsberg bridges, to the subject of graph theory. A **graph** is a system of dots, **vertices** or **nodes**, connected by lines, or **edges**. Two graphs are considered the same, or topologically equivalent, if corresponding nodes are joined in corresponding ways. However, the exact position of the nodes or shape of the edges is unimportant; only the pattern of connections matters.

Graphs embody in an abstract form the 'skeleton' of many complex problems. For example, the nodes may represent the various tasks that must be performed in manufacturing a certain product; and the edges may link tasks, one of which is a prerequisite for the other. By analysing the graph, the most efficient ordering of the tasks may be deduced. Again, the nodes may represent components in an electronic circuit, and the edges the wires that connect them. The graph can be used to seek the best arrangement of components on a circuit board.

Graphs provide a simple example of the power of a mathematical abstraction to strip away inessentials and leave only the key elements of structure. Euler's decisive work on traversing a graph along every edge is one early application. There are many others, including the arrangements of chemical bonds in complex molecules, as well as purely mathematical problems. An analogous problem to Euler's theory is the Hamiltonian Problem: when is it possible to find a path through a graph that visits each node exactly once (but need not traverse every edge)? The Travelling Salesman Problem is much the same: the nodes are cities, the edges roads; the problem here is to make the total distance as short as possible.

Neither the Hamiltonian Problem nor that of the Travelling Salesman is fully solved, even now. A delightful puzzle based on the former is Hamilton's Icosian Game, presented here as the Galaxy Game.

	Path	Cycle	Star	Tree	Wheel
2					
3					
4					
5					
6					

Five important families of simple graphs

A simple graph is one that has no self-loops (lines that join a point to itself).

Many simple graphs have names like 'path', 'cycle', 'star', 'tree', 'wheel', etc.

Complete graphs on two to six points

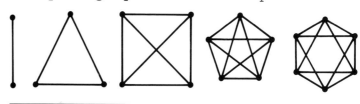

Galaxy game ▷

A puzzle game based on the Hamiltonian Problem. Cut out twenty discs numbered from 1 to 20 to play the game, the rules of which are:

1 To visit all circles (planets) in one continuous trip by placing discs on them one at a time

2 To place the discs in the number sequence of 1 to 20.

3 Start at any point you wish, visit every circle once, but you must return to the start at the end of your trip

(Solution: page 113)

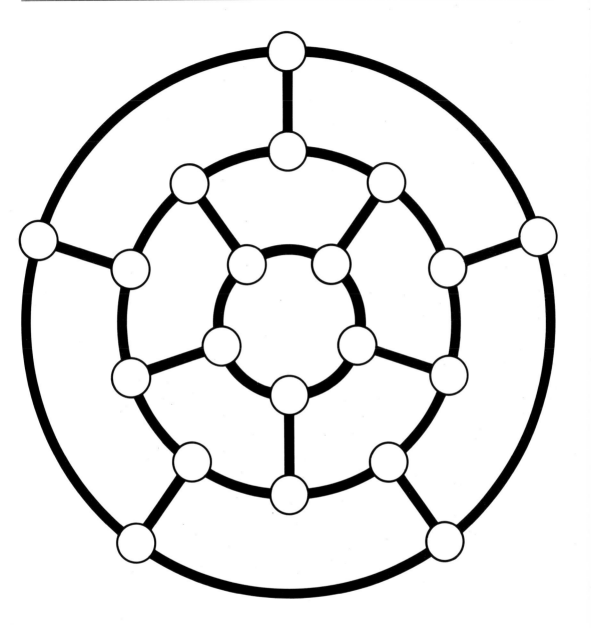

If a graph can be drawn on the plane without its edges crossing (other than at a node), then it is said to be **planar**. For example, the graph formed by the components of an electrical circuit on one side of a printed circuit board must be planar, to avoid short circuits. (In practice, however, connections on both sides of the board can be used to avoid crossings.)

The complete graph with four nodes ('complete' meaning that all pairs are joined by an edge) is planar. The complete graph on five nodes is **not** planar, a result that can be deduced from some geometrical ideas of Euler. The graph for the Utilities Problem has six nodes

arranged in two sets of three: any node in one set is connected to all nodes in the other. Is the graph planar? That is, can the utility companies connect up the houses without getting their connections tangled?

The answer is no.

In fact a theorem of Kuratowski shows that a graph is planar exactly if (and only if) it does not contain within itself a graph that is either:

[a] the complete graph on five nodes

[b] the utilities graph.

Edwin Abbott wrote a remarkable and charming piece of mathematical science fiction called **Flatland**, in which polygonal creatures

inhabit a planar universe (and suggestions of a world of three dimensions are rank heresy). Intelligent Flatlanders, however, appear to be ruled out by graph theory. If their brains had more than four cells, it would not be possible to interconnect them all by nerves. Designing a brain, or an electronic computer, in Flatland would be a taxing task. Unless, perhaps, some technological or biological device could be found to allow connections to cross – much as traffic lights or level crossings permit intersections of roads and railway lines.

Von Neumann's cellular automata (see page 86) might provide an answer.

A planar graph on four points

The utilities problem

Each house must receive gas, water and electricity. Can lines be drawn to connect each house with each utility in such a way that no lines intersect?

Would all Flatlanders get gas, water and electricity?

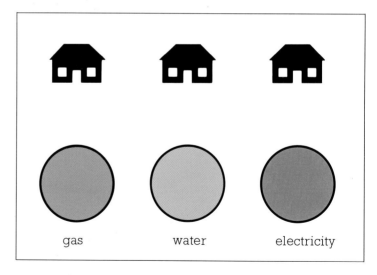

gas   water   electricity

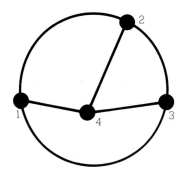

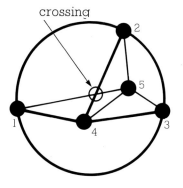

crossing

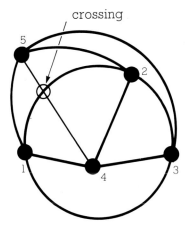

crossing

Complete graphs on five points

Visual proof that the complete graph on five points has a crossing number of 1

If edges are permitted to cross at points other than nodes, then any graph may be drawn in the plane. Such an 'unintended' meeting of two edges is a **crossing point**. Topological deformation of a graph may **change** the number of crossings: for example, the complete graph on four nodes can be drawn as a square plus its diagonals, with nodes at its corners. The intersection of the diagonals is a crossing in this sense. The same graph can be drawn in the plane, avoiding all crossings, as on the left.

Of all the ways of drawing a given graph in the plane, there is at least one that has fewer crossings than any other. This **minimal** number of crossings is called, naturally enough, the **crossing number**, and it is now a topological invariant. Graphs with crossing number 0 are planar graphs. The crossing number is remarkably difficult to

calculate, and it is not known in general even for complete graphs. It is 1 for the complete graph with five nodes, by Kuratowski's Theorem.

A **complete bipartite** graph is a generalized version of the utilities graph. Its nodes are divided into two sets, with m and n nodes each. All nodes in one set are joined to all nodes in the other set; but no two nodes in the same set are joined. For the utilities graph $(m=n=3)$. the crossing number is 1.
Again the crossing number for general m and n is not known. For example, if $m=n=7$, then it **is** known that the crossing number is either 77, 79 or 81. But nobody knows which of these three is the correct answer!
Many other simple properties of graphs prove equally elusive. Combinatorial mathematics is still in its infancy.

The four-school problem

As you will see, this is a $m=4$, $n=4$ type problem.
Four schoolboys live in four different houses and go to four different schools.
Lead each of them to his school without any of their paths crossing

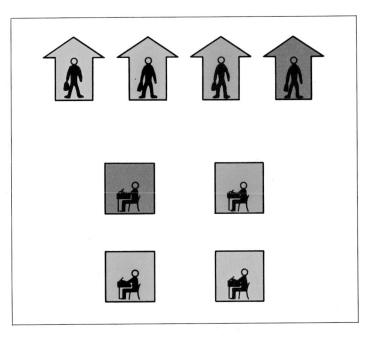

24 Tree graphs

Topology has become a cornerstone of modern mathematics. In topology we are concerned with those properties of a figure that remain unchanged under continuous deformations. Examples of properties that are **not** topological include the angles of a triangle – by deforming the triangle it is possible to make the angles change. Similarly the lengths of the sides are not topological properties. Indeed **being** a triangle is not a topological property: by introducing a bend in one side of a triangle, it can be continuously deformed into a quadrilateral. In fact, to a topologist, a triangle is the same as a square, a parallelogram – even a circle! Clearly little traditional geometry survives from the topological viewpoint.

So what properties **are** topological? The fact that a triangle has an inside and an outside, and that it is impossible to pass from one to the other without crossing an edge of the triangle, is a topological property. No matter how a triangle is deformed in the plane, it will still possess an inside and an outside. The fact that a car inner tube has a hole in the middle is a topological property; even a very distorted tube retains its hole. Many topological properties have to do with the way objects are or are not connected up. Whether or not a loop of string is knotted is a topological property. The basic concepts of topology include many ideas we learn as infants: insideness and outsideness, right- and left-handedness, linking, knotting, connectedness and disconnectedness. Topology, in a precise sense, is the science of the **qualitative**.

Two figures are said to be **topologically equivalent** if one can be continuously deformed into another. So a sphere and a cube are topologically equivalent; and the figure 8 and the letter B are topologically equivalent (each has two holes). A fundamental problem in topology is to classify objects into classes of topologically equivalent things.

Topology is very basic and fundamental. During the last thirty years or so it has been applied to problems in mechanics, chemistry, physics, symbolic logic, weather prediction, magnetism, biology and psychology.

A simple area where topological ideas arise is the theory of graphs. When nodes are joined by edges what matters is not the precise **position** of the edges and nodes – it is **the way they connect up**. For example, a graph is **connected** if it is 'all in one piece', which means that there exists a continuous path from any node to any other. The precise shape of the edges is irrelevant; connectedness is topological in character. Similarly, if a graph contains a **circuit** – a closed loop of distinct edges – then so does any topologically equivalent graph. In some ways the simplest graphs are those that contain no circuits. These are called **trees** because while they often branch, the branches never link up again.

We can also start with a set of labelled nodes and ask how many different trees can **span** (that is, connect) them. With four points there are sixteen trees. In general, as we discuss elsewhere, n points can be spanned by n^{n-2} trees. We show the different topological types of tree that can be formed using up to seven nodes.

Many processes that branch may be represented as trees. For example, the positions in a game of chess form a tree whose edges are the moves of the game. The theory of strategy in games is generally based on viewing the game as a tree; and computer programs that play games such as chess, draughts, or backgammon, make essential use of this idea.

Trees are a traditional symbol of

Spanning tree graphs

The sixteen trees that span four points

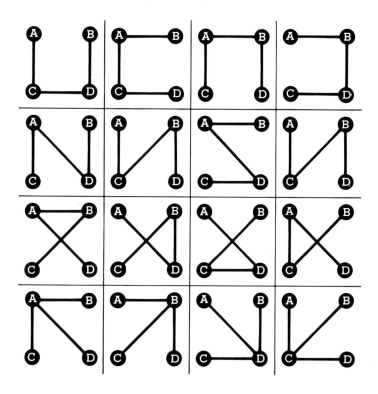

life and growth. They occur in early attempts to represent logical relations diagrammatically. They were known to Aristotle. Ancient and medieval philosophers were obsessed with tree graphs (much as many modern sociologists are obsessed with graphs in general) and these are still widely used to classify objects in hierarchical systems. The classification of living creatures into phyla, genera, species, etc., is an example. Porphyry, a thirteenth-century Roman philosopher, proposed the 'tree of Porphyry', which is essentially what is today called a **binary tree** (at the most, two branches occur at any node). Any series of 'yes/no' questions (such as often used in classifying things or in computer circuits) leads to a binary tree.

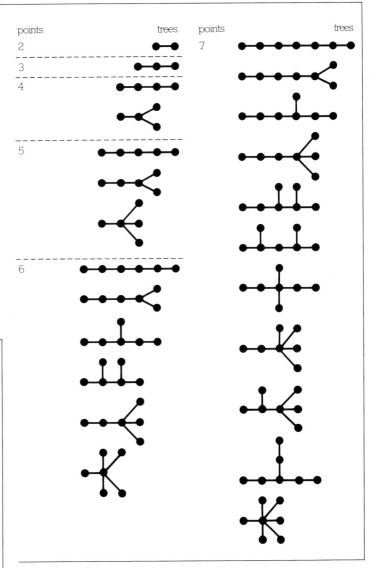

Topologically distinct trees of two up to seven points

A B C D
E F G H
I J K L M
N O P Q
R S T U
V W X
Y Z

◁The topology of the alphabet

Which of the letters are trees?
Which letters are topologically equivalent?

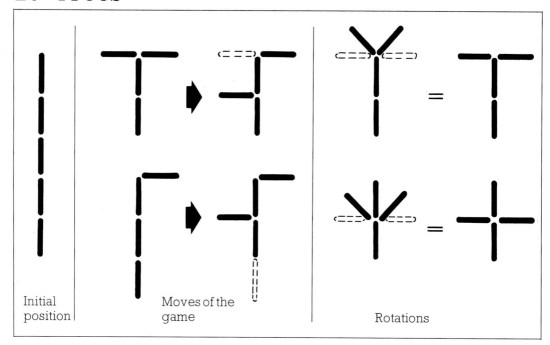

Initial position | Moves of the game | Rotations

Trees

Moves and rotations

The idea of topological equivalence is fundamental to modern mathematics, applied as well as pure. Understanding and recognition of this concept should be a must for everybody.

Trees, a simple and extremely rewarding party game for two or more players, is designed to encourage such understanding. It is both an elegant and attractive game, and an educational aid.

The game of Trees requires the following equipment:

[a] a set of cards, depicting stylized versions of a selection of tree graphs with three, four, five and six nodes

[b] a set of six sticks, used in the game to recreate the graphs shown on the cards.

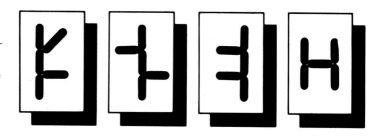

Cards for playing Trees

A set of topologically equivalent cards (a six-point graph in four different transformations)

Rules of the game

Object: to collect the highest score, by using the sticks to form the graphs shown on the cards.

HOW TO PLAY

Shuffle the cards and place them face down in a pile.
Place five sticks in a straight line on the table. The sixth stick is held in reserve.
The first player takes the top three cards from the pile and places them face up. He or she then has **two** moves (explained below) to change the positions of the sticks to match the graphs shown on the exposed cards.
If a player succeeds in forming such a graph, he takes that card and keeps it till the end of the game.

MOVES

There are three basic moves:
1 Pick up a stick from the table and lay it in a new position.
2 Add a stick from the reserve.
3 Remove a stick and place it in reserve.
However, a player may also make as many **rotations** as required, where a rotation takes the following form:
4 Pivot a stick about one of its ends, provided this end is attached to the remainder of the graph. A stick that is attached at both ends may not rotate.
Rotations do **not** count towards the player's two-move total; but cards may be picked up if the corresponding shape is formed after a rotation or a series of rotations.
The second player now takes

enough cards from the pile to make the exposed cards up to three once more, and plays in exactly the same way.
The game continues until all the cards have been taken. The winner is the player with the most cards.

VARIATIONS

There are two forms of the game: classical and topological.
In the classical game, a card may only be taken if the tree formed by the sticks is exactly the same as that depicted on the card.
In the topological game, it may be taken if the trees are topologically equivalent.
By playing both versions of the game, it is possible to gain an excellent idea of the difference between exact similarity and topological equivalence.

Trees sample

Top: three cards facing up at the beginning of a player's turn.
Bottom: the player's moves resulting in getting all three cards, i.e. a score of 3 points

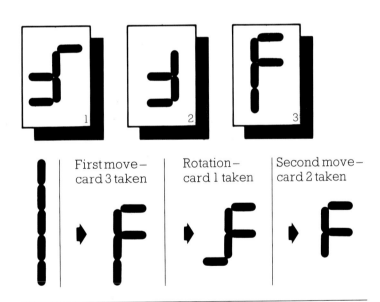

First move –
card 3 taken

Rotation –
card 1 taken

Second move –
card 2 taken

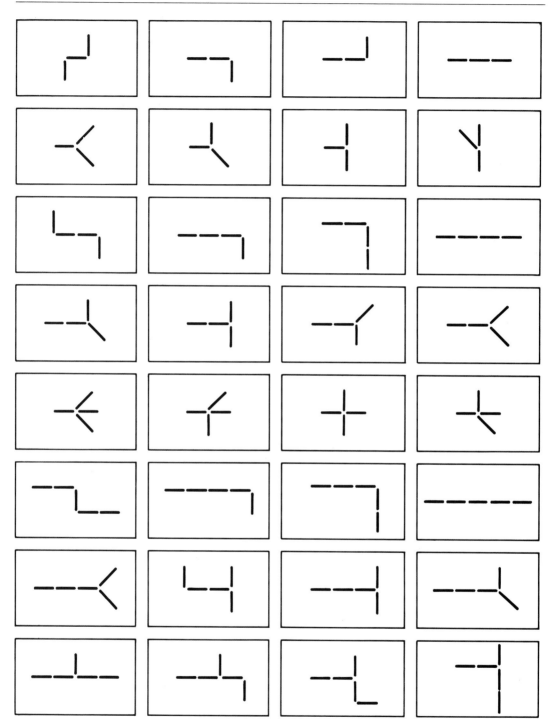

The full set of Trees cards

A set of sixteen topologically inequivalent cards, each
coming in four topologically equivalent variations, giving
sixty-four cards altogether

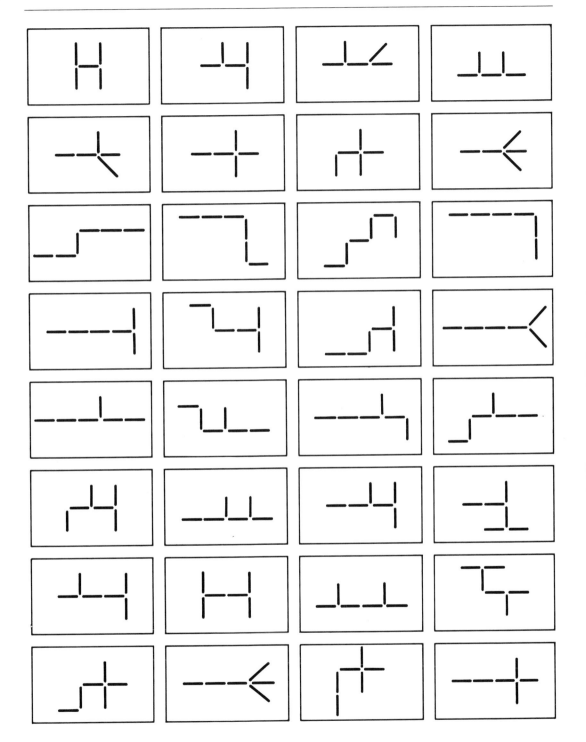

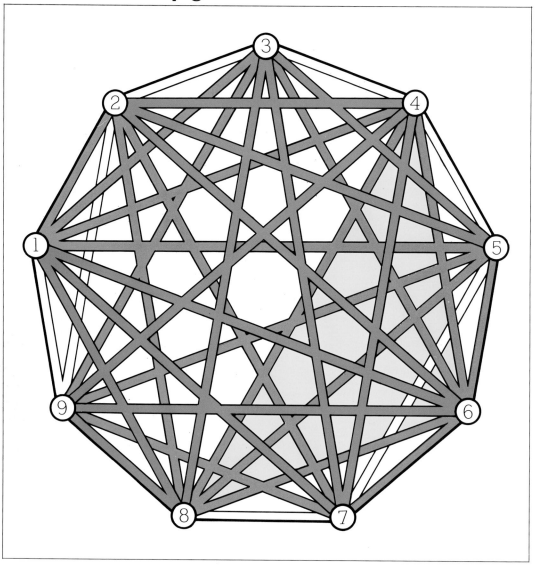

Many problems require that the edges of a graph be distinguished from each other by the assignment of labels. An attractive way to do this is to colour the edges. We may ask how many colours are necessary to satisfy certain preassigned conditions – for example, that no edges meeting at a given node have the same colour.

Can a complete graph have its edges coloured, using only **two** colours, so that no three edges of the same colour form a triangle? The cases with four nodes (answer: yes) and five (no) are simple enough to analyse by hand. Can

you find a solution for four nodes? Can you prove that no solution exists for five?

Some general theorems of this type were proved by Ramsey, and our graph-colouring game is named after him. Two players (red and blue) take it in turns to colour single edges of a complete graph with nine nodes. The first to be forced to form a closed triangle with edges all the same colour **loses**. The game can be played using the accompanying board, coloured pens and transparent paper.

The Ramsey game on a complete graph on nine points

The player playing the red pen lost by being forced to close a red triangle (yellow area).

Try to play the game with other complete graphs

Ramsey game board
Put a transparent paper overlay on the board – so you can play the game again

The tangram dissection
scheme

If two plane figures with straight-line edges (polygons, regular or irregular) can be assembled from the same set of pieces by fitting them together in different ways, then it is clear that the **areas** of the two figures are the same.

Conversely, it can also be shown that any two polygons of equal area may be dissected into a finite number of pieces, which may be assembled to form either of the two original polygons.

In dissection problems, the pieces may be already given; the object is to create as many interesting patterns as possible with them. The ancient recreation of the **tangram** is an example.

On the other hand, only the two polygons may be given; then the problem is to find ways to dissect them. Usually the object is to use as few pieces as possible.

A third, apparently paradoxical, variant is to dissect a shape into pieces, remove one piece, and re-assemble the remainder to form the original shape. On grounds of area this is impossible; despite this, the Mystrix puzzle (see page 47) appears to achieve it. How?

Jigsaw puzzles are dissection puzzles of yet another (and less interesting) type, in which the required assembly is unique. Dissections are typical of many simple but subtle problems where there is no obvious starting point, 'nothing to get hold of'. This is what makes them both difficult and challenging. In 1900 the famous mathematician David Hilbert gave an address in Paris, at which he listed twenty-three outstanding mathematical problems. Many of these still tax our ingenuity, but one was solved within a year by Max Dehn. Hilbert asked whether two polyhedral solids of equal **volume** can always be dissected into a system of identical pieces (and conjectured that they could not). Dehn proved his guess correct.

Volume is more subtle than area.

The tangram

The oldest known mathematical dissection puzzle is the ancient Chinese tangram puzzle.
There are dozens of variations of the tangram, but in its original form it is probably still the best puzzle in its category.
It is a rewarding challenge to re-create the limitless variety of pictures with the tangram shapes – abstracts as well as figurative shapes.

Right: figurative problem samples
Far right: abstract problem samples, which are usually more difficult than the figurative shapes

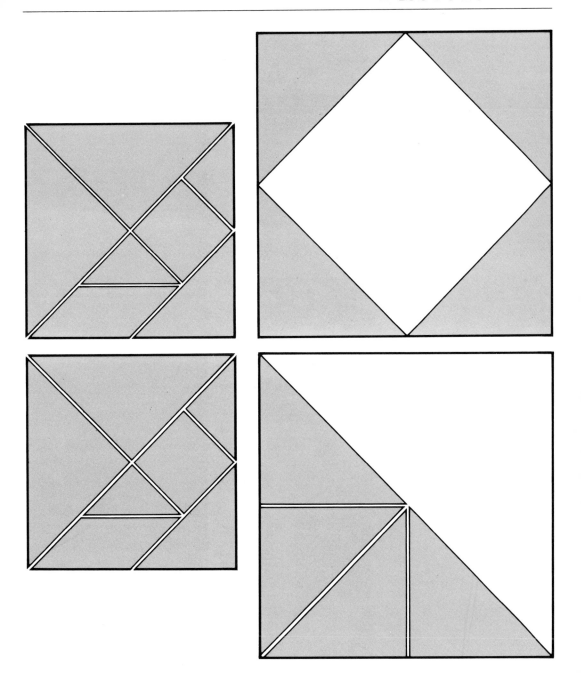

Double tangram puzzle

Copy and cut out two identical sets of tangrams (left).
Complete the two big squares illustrated (right).
Each square is the same area as the two tangrams, and in each of them the four big triangles have already been placed

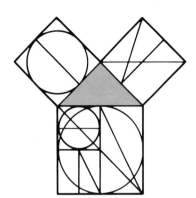

The structure

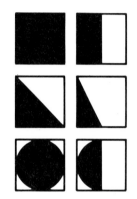

The six shapes

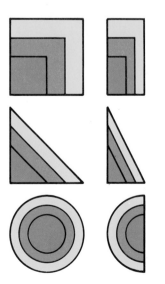

The three sizes
and colours

Toys, houses, flowers, cars, churches, flags, people, children, boats, swimming pools, cows, dolls, horses, ducks, donkeys, space rockets.... The world of even the youngest child is filled with almost endless variety, a world of strange and exciting objects.

It is a vital part of the child's education that he should learn to relate these objects to himself and to each other; to distinguish them by their features; to know which are safe and which are to be avoided. But where is he to start? What do such widely different things have in common?

They all have shape. They all have size. They can all be counted. They all have colour. Many of them move. Many of them grow.... From these underlying elements of shape, size, number, colour, movement and growth, the child can be led to discover many of the basic ideas of mathematics and to relate them to his own familiar world.

The Shape Family Programme is designed for children in nursery school and early infant school. But its usefulness does not always end there. In one inner city New York school it has been welcomed enthusiastically and used by children up to the age of eleven.

It has only six basic elements: square, rectangle, circle, semi-circle and two types of triangle. Each comes in three different sizes and three different colours.

The Pythagorean Theorem lurks in the background as a major theme.

A Pythagorean ▷ world of fun

Using a limited number of shapes, you can create all kinds of things ... a whole universe

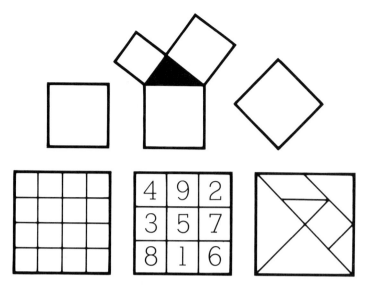

'It's a square!
Beautiful!
Equilateral! and
Rectangular!'

(Lewis Carroll)

The square is the simplest, most symmetrical and most perfect quadrilateral. Its sides are all equal, its angles all right angles. But its simplicity is deceptive. The square conceals within its austere geometry untold intellectual depths. It is **static** when resting on one of its sides, **dynamic** when balanced on one of its angles. It is a **matrix** and a **lattice** when divided into its unit squares. It is **magic** when filled with numbers in special configurations. In its lifelong partnership with the right-angled triangle it features as the principal character in the Pythagorean drama, the inspiration for more mathematics than most of us are aware exists. From Pythagoras's Theorem to Einstein's Theory of General Relativity, from the flat geometry of Euclid to the curvature of space, is but three or four short steps, with the square as their common thread.

The square is found in nature in the crystals of many minerals, including common salt. It has provided the proportions of famous ancient structures and modern buildings. It played a role in the structure of the Hebrew alphabet.

The square has given birth to many ancient games that are still played today: chess, Go, solitaire, dominoes. And to many new games that have yet to be created.

Square dissections

All the patterns are based on bisection or trisection of the sides of the squares. Therefore they can easily be drawn, coloured and cut out to become twelve dissection puzzles. To re-create the original squares from their parts will not be so easy

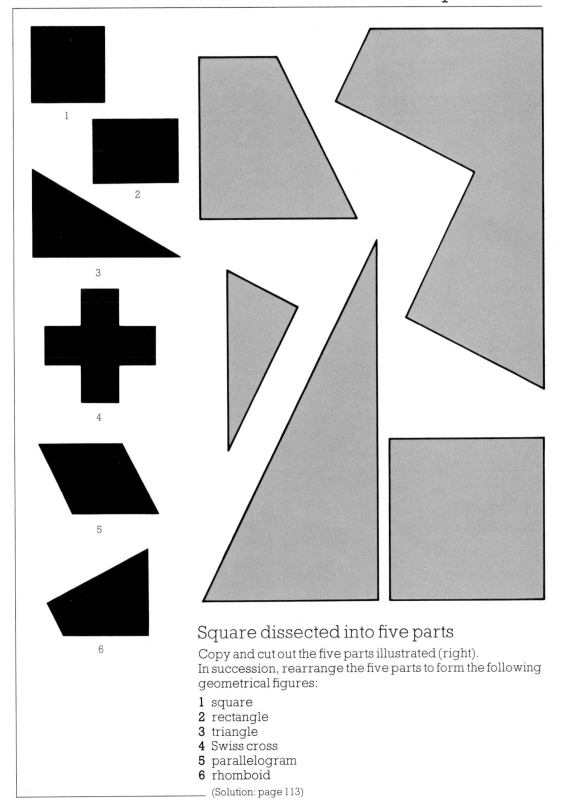

Square dissected into five parts

Copy and cut out the five parts illustrated (right).
In succession, rearrange the five parts to form the following geometrical figures:

1 square
2 rectangle
3 triangle
4 Swiss cross
5 parallelogram
6 rhomboid

(Solution: page 113)

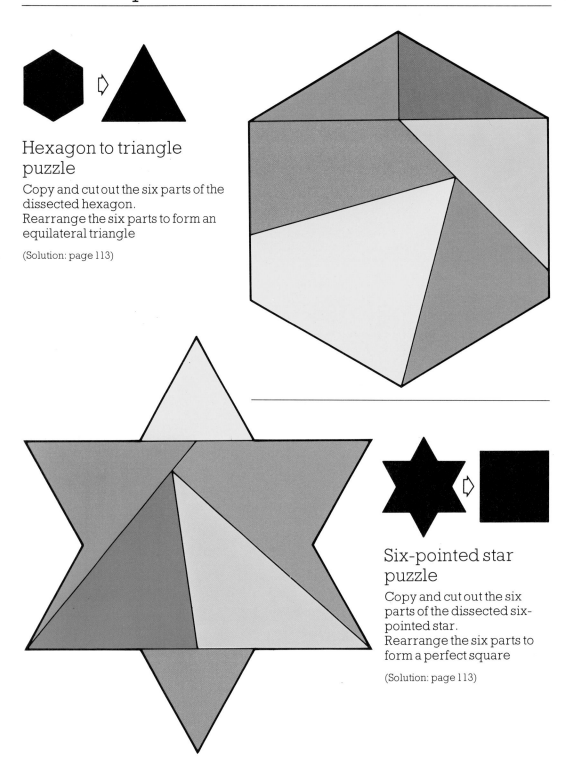

Hexagon to triangle puzzle

Copy and cut out the six parts of the dissected hexagon.
Rearrange the six parts to form an equilateral triangle

(Solution: page 113)

Six-pointed star puzzle

Copy and cut out the six parts of the dissected six-pointed star.
Rearrange the six parts to form a perfect square

(Solution: page 113)

Stars puzzle

Copy and cut out the twenty-four parts of the twelve-pointed star. Rearrange the twenty-four pieces to form three identical smaller replicas of the big star

(Solution: page 113)

40 Square packing

Packing problems are not just intellectual games. 'Wheels within wheels' is a common enough phrase – but what of squares within squares? Suppose you are given a number of identical unit-sized squares to pack inside a larger square. What is the smallest size that the large square can be to be able to fit **n** unit squares into it without overlaps?

If the squares are not allowed to tilt, the problem becomes a good deal simpler. The most difficult case is that of tilted squares.

Of the potential infinity of possible arrangements, which is the most efficient?

For **n** = 1, 2, 3, 4, tilting provides no advantage. When **n** = 5, it is possible to tilt all five squares to form a cross. But a more efficient packing is obtained if only the central square is tilted: the larger square has side 2.707. Without tilting, the best possible would be 3.

For **n** = 6, 7, 8 and 9, again the untilted solution is as efficient as any other.

For **n** = 10 and 11, it is certainly necessary to tilt; but nobody knows if the solutions so far obtained are the best, or whether some ingenious packing can be made to do better. For larger values of **n**, virtually nothing is known.

There are many other packing problems, most of which are equally baffling, especially those that allow irregular packing. An important example is the packing of circles in the plane. Take a large number of identical coins, and arrange some of them in a line, touching one another. Now add coins on either side, touching these in pairs, forming rows of coins that are staggered so that each coin is surrounded by six others. This is **hexagonal lattice packing**.

It is fairly easy to show that it is the most efficient regular packing of circles. It is enormously harder (though it has been done none the less) to show that no irregular packing can be denser.

The analogous problem of spheres packed into space poses more severe problems still. The densest regular packing is known; but whether any irregular packing can do better is a mystery. The best guess is no, but that remains unproved.

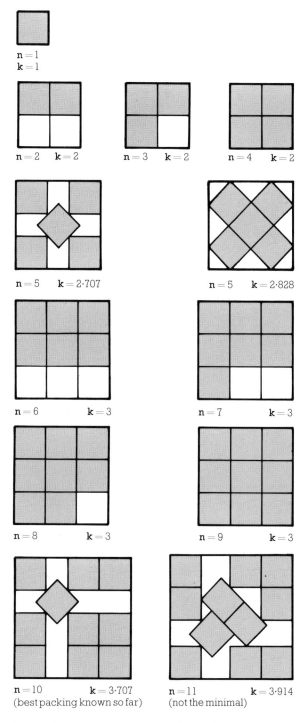

Packing squares with unit squares

The first twelve solutions, up to eleven squares

Packing squares with eleven unit squares

Copy and cut out exactly eleven unit squares.
The eleven unit squares have to be packed into the square area.
There are two rules for the packing:

1 No parts of the eleven unit squares are allowed to trespass onto the black outline.

2 No overlapping of the unit squares is allowed.

Seems impossible? Try harder

(Solution: page 114)

unit square

42 A strange coincidence

We may also ask about packing non-identical squares. One possibility that springs to mind is to use squares of side 1, 2, 3, 4 ... and so on, up to some particular limit. Can a large square be cut up into such a system of smaller squares? Squares of sides 1 and 2 cannot form a square: the best they can do is fit inside a square of side 3 leaving an empty space. Similarly squares of sides 1, 2, 3 cannot fill a square; nor 1, 2, 3, 4.

If the squares are to fill the large square completely, then they cannot be placed at a tilt. So the outer square must have a side that is a whole number. Therefore the total area of the system of small squares must itself be a perfect square. But

$$1^2 + 2^2 = 5,$$
$$1^2 + 2^2 + 3^2 = 14,$$
$$1^2 + 2^2 + 3^2 + 4^2 = 30.$$

None of these are perfect squares. Continuing the calculation, we find eventually that

$$1^2 + 2^2 + 3^2 + \ldots 24^2 = 4900 = 70^2.$$

In fact, this is the **only** way to add consecutive squares and obtain a square for the total. (The demonstration is a difficult exercise in the theory of numbers, and was itself an unsolved problem for a considerable time.)

This raises the following geometrical variation: is it possible to pack squares of sides 1, 2, 3 ... 24 into the 70×70 square? Equality of areas is a necessary condition – but might not be sufficient. One might expect the answer to be yes – why else the remarkable coincidence for the 70×70 square? But in fact it is no. The problem must therefore be rephrased: how many of the system of squares is it possible to pack into the 70×70 square. The best answer known to date is 'all but one', and in every known example it is the 7×7 square that must be left out.

Twenty-four distinct solutions of this kind exist, but it is still not known if a better way of packing can be found, omitting squares of a smaller total area than $7 \times 7 = 49$. To tackle this beautiful problem, cut out from stiff cardboard a set of twenty-four consecutive squares,

of sides 1 cm up to 24 cm. Now draw a 70×70 cm square and rule it into unit squares. Try to place as many of the cardboard squares as you can, without overlaps.

Another variation: given a set of consecutive squares, what is the smallest rectangle (in total area) into which they will fit? The case of eleven squares is particularly interesting, because of a curious spiral arrangement which breaks down at the twelfth square. Again, it is possible to experiment with cutout cardboard squares.

Exhaustive enumeration of all possible arrangements would take far too long, even on a fast computer, for most such problems. Trial-and-error experiment can find solutions, if they exist; but to eliminate possibilities altogether requires more cunning trickery ... in short, a genuine **idea**.

All these problems can be made into competitive games for two persons. Players take it in turn to place squares within the boundary; the first unable to move loses. Here are two more questions about the set of twenty-four squares.
1 Can the odd-sided squares be fitted into a 48×48 square?
2 Can the even-sided squares be fitted into a 51×51 square?

SIDE	AREA	SUM
1	1	1
2	4	5
3	9	14
4	16	30
5	25	55
6	36	91
7	49	140
8	64	204
9	81	285
10	100	385
11	121	506
12	144	650
13	169	819
14	196	1015
15	225	1240
16	256	1496
17	289	1785
18	324	2109
19	361	2470
20	400	2870
21	441	3311
22	484	3795
23	529	4324
24	576	4900
Total area		4900

Sums of the first twenty-four square numbers

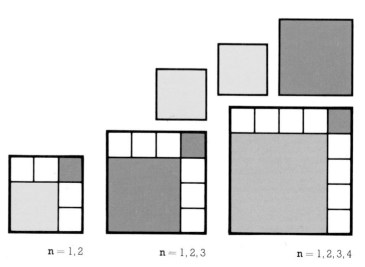

n = 1, 2   n = 1, 2, 3   n = 1, 2, 3, 4

The square-packing problem
For the first 2, 3 and 4 consecutive squares

Squares infinity – eleven squares

The first of eleven squares in the 30 × 25 rectangle. It is interesting to see that the first eleven consecutive squares can be spiralled around a centre forming a 30 × 25 rectangle.

If we try to add the next, side 12, square, there would be an enclosed hole in the configuration

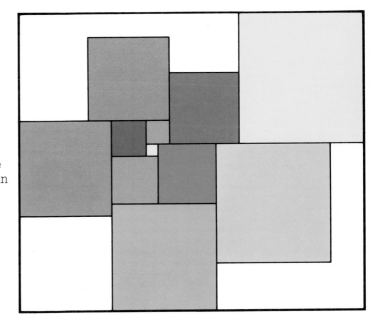

Squares infinity – twenty-four squares

One of the minimal solutions with the 7 × 7 square outside the 70 × 70 board

Squares infinity

Three-dimensional free-play
activity

Of course, we do not have to insist that all the small squares be different. We could allow repetitions of the same size. Given a large square of size **n**, what is the smallest number of squares (of whole-number side) into which it can be split?

For instance, a 3×3 square divides into one 2×2 square and five 1×1 squares, a total of **six** pieces. The larger 4×4 square could be divided into one 3×3 and seven 1×1s, a total of eight pieces ... but it could also be divided into four 2×2s, which is far better. In general, even values of **n** have a simple answer (can you find it?), but the problem is much more subtle for odd **n**. You can experiment using the grids on the right.

Imperfect squares

Imperfect squares are squares which can be subdivided into smaller squares, two or more of which can be alike.

The matrices of the first thirteen imperfect squares, of order 1 to order 13, are illustrated (having sides of 1 to 13 units).

Subdivide them into the smallest possible number of square elements

(Solution: page 114)

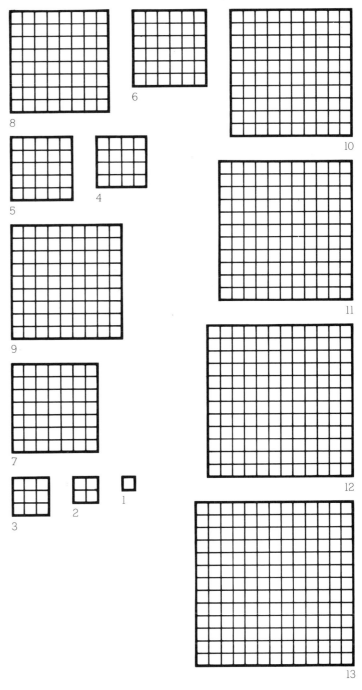

Although the 70×70 square cannot be split into twenty-four subsquares of sides 1, 2, ... 24, the number 24 figures in another square-dissection problem.

Say that a rectangle or square is **perfect** if it can be cut into a set of smaller squares whose sides are all different. (All sides here should be whole numbers.) Perfect rectangles are relatively easy to find. In fact the 32×33 rectangle (very nearly a square) divides exactly into squares of sides 1, 4, 7, 8, 9, 10, 14, 15, 18.

Can you work out how?

It follows that it is impossible to divide a rectangle into fewer than nine different squares.

For a long time it was not known whether any perfect **squares** (in this sense) could exist. Eventually a team of mathematicians, exploiting an analogy with the theory of electrical circuits, found such a square. The best known solution requires twenty-four squares (but not of consecutive sizes!) and is illustrated here. Can you work out what the sides must be?

We end our discussion of squares with a paradox. A square may be dissected into seventeen parts. If one of these parts is discarded, the remaining sixteen may be rearranged to fill the original square. Or doesn't that sound right? Try it. Then explain it.

The smallest perfect square

A set of twenty-four different squares forming the smallest perfect square

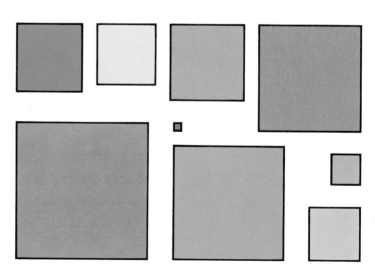

The smallest perfect rectangle

Copy and cut out the nine squares and use them to create the smallest perfect rectangle

(Solution: page 115)

Mystrix

Copy the picture and cut it into seventeen parts along the thin dividing lines. Obviously, it is possible to assemble all seventeen parts to make the original square – although this is not so easy without the diagram. Now **remove** one of the five small square pieces ... and assemble the rest to fill up the square again. Surely this can't be done, because the area is less; but if you try hard, you'll find a solution

(Solution: page 115)

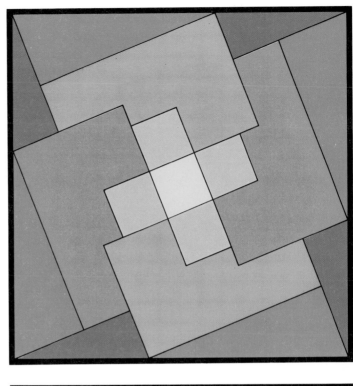

If a line is drawn across a square, passing through the centre, it produces two identical pieces. Other shapes may also be bisected by a single line. A variety of shapes is shown here for you to find the bisectors. Their lines can be curved or straight; the only condition is that a **single** line is used. It may be necessary to rotate one of the two halves to match the shapes up. A square may also be quartered by drawing two perpendicular lines through its centre. When you have solved the bisection problems, try to quarter the shapes shown here. The grid lines are intended only as an aid to visualization. It is not necessarily the case that the lines you need will follow the grid lines. Of course, sometimes they may!

Bisection problems

Here are five shapes to be divided exactly in two by a single line. The two parts must be the same shape and size, that is, **congruent**.

The grid lines are drawn as aids to visualization, but it is **not** necessary to make cuts along the grid lines. You may cut anywhere you wish

(Solution: page 115)

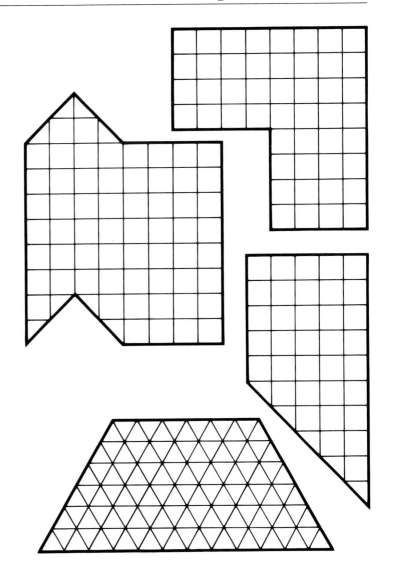

Quartering problems

A collection of four shapes which have to be cut into four congruent quarters

(Solution: page 115)

50 Polygo

Jigsaw puzzles, we said earlier, are relatively uninteresting dissection puzzles. So here is a jigsaw with a difference.

Polygo is a puzzle game for two or more players, based on the creation and recognition of complex polygons – built up from only four simple basic shapes:

TRIANGLE   PENTAGON
SQUARE   HEXAGON

By assembling these, it is possible to construct fifty different polygons (not counting rotations).

The game is played with twenty-four tiles. On each tile the four basic shapes occur in different combi-

nations and different colours. By copying the diagram opposite, make a set of tiles out of card, and colour them with paint or marker pen.

The object of the game is to create complex polygons of uniform colour, by placing tiles side by side. Each such polygon, when completed, has a score value shown in the accompanying chart.

First, each player chooses a colour. Different players much choose different colours.

The tiles are laid face down and mixed thoroughly. Players take turns to draw a tile and place it on the table adjacent to the tiles already

laid. The game continues until all tiles have been used. Each player adds up the scores of the completed polygons of his colour. (Each such polygon will be formed from four tiles, placed in a square, with the four touching corners all having the same colour.) The player with the highest total wins.

Note that the more complicated the polygon, the greater the score. To play the game well, you must recognize the polygons.

You can also play a solitaire version of the game. Can you assemble all twenty-four tiles in a 6 × 4 rectangle so that all colours match when two tiles are adjacent?

Score chart

The complex polygons created from combinations of four basic shapes are scored according to the following principle:
TRIANGLES value 1
SQUARES value 2
PENTAGONS value 3
HEXAGONS value 4
Thus, the simplest complex polygon created will have a value of 4, and the highest a value of 16

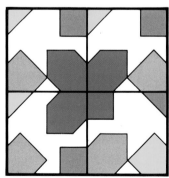

Game sample

Four tiles forming a violet complex polygon of value 14

Game tiles ▷

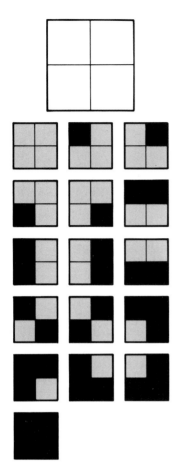

In modern computers, information is represented by **bits** – the digits 0 and 1. You can think of a bit as the state of a switch: 0 means 'off' and 1 means 'on'. With four switches there will be two possibilities each, making a total of
$2 \times 2 \times 2 \times 2 = 16$
ways to set them.

If we represent the switches as four square cells, arranged in a 2×2 square, and colour the 'off' switches white and the 'on' switches black, we obtain a set of sixteen tiles that can be used to play a game. In fact, several.

There are many different ways to arrange the sixteen tiles in a 4×4 square. But is it possible to do this in such a way that the colours of adjacent tiles match everywhere? Make a set of tiles and try. In fact there are quite a few solutions; about fifty are known to date.

Bits solutions

Here are twelve solutions of the bits colour-matching puzzle. How many different solutions are there altogether? Remember, rotations, reflections, or solutions where the colours are just swapped round should not be considered different from each other

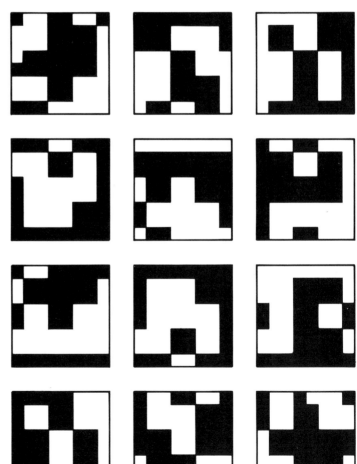

Two-colouring of square matrices

Let's take a square, colour it black or white – there will be two possibilities.

Take two squares – four different patterns will be possible.

Following the same procedure with three squares – eight different patterns will be created.

Using four unit squares in a 2×2 configuration we can create sixteen different patterns

Two players can play this in competition. Give each a complete set of sixteen tiles and squared paper to record any solution found. See who can discover the most in a given time.

The sixteen tiles are composed of sixty-four unit squares. Half of these are black, half white. By assembling them to make the colours match – we shall call this the **domino principle** – we create merging zones of the two different colours, dividing the whole into separate fields of colour.

By using a scoring system for solutions that depend on the number of fields so created, we can give weight to solutions producing a more complicated final pattern. (Fields that touch only at a single point, across a corner, should be considered different.) Two players can compete, each forming a pattern and seeing who scores the highest.

Bits board game

If as well as the tiles we make an 8 × 8 square board, such that each tile fits exactly on four of its squares, we can play a rewarding two-player game with very simple rules. Place the tiles face down and mix them thoroughly. In turn, each player must take a tile and place it on the board. It must fit over exactly four of the squares on the board. If it touches any other tiles along an edge or half an edge, the colours must match. (Note that tiles may be placed with only half an edge in common if one is displaced a single row from the other. See the sample game.) The first player unable to place his tile is the loser. The longest that such a game can go on is sixteen moves – ending with a solution to the original problem that started this section. What is the shortest possible game? That is, if a single player plays solitaire, and selects from the sixteen tiles laid face up, what is the smallest number of tiles needed to block the board, so that no others can be laid?

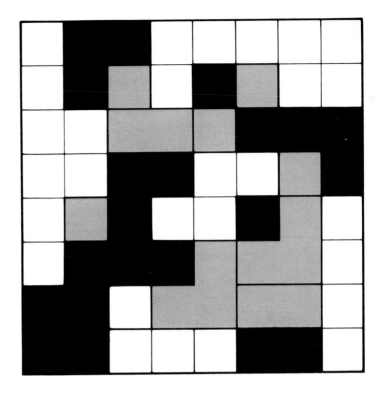

Bits board game sample
A game finished in nine moves

Bits creative craft activity

Re-create these illustrations using square two-colour
tiles of only four basic kinds. Copy and cut out about
thirty of each tile. Try to create compositions of your
own using backgrounds of different colours

Tiles need not be square. In particular, they can be hexagonal, a fact known to bees who base the designs for their honeycomb upon hexagonal tiling. Perhaps the hive could use hexabits to teach young bees about computers? The set of nineteen hexagons represent all the distinct ways of dividing a hexagon into black and white (two-colour) areas, by connecting their vertices with straight lines. Copy and cut out the set of nineteen hexagons. The object of the game is to fit all the hexagons to form the honeycomb configuration – so that all the touching edges match in colour.

Hexabits puzzle solution

Can you find another solution?

Hexabits

Dissection structure

58 Transclown

From computers to clowns; from the abstract to the friendly. Who would believe that a simple 4×4 matrix could reveal such a variety? Transclown is a game of a thousand faces, offering fascinating opportunities for creative play, puzzles and games for all ages.

Take a 4×4 matrix. Draw upon it the simplest face you can make using only a ruler and a compass – that is Transclown.

Copy the diagram, paint it, and cut into sixteen tiles along the grid lines. The grid has been chosen so that when the tiles are rearranged, many pleasing patterns result. If the tiles are kept in the same orientation – that is, not rotated – there are

$16 \times 15 \times 14 \times 13 \times 12 \times 11 \times 10 \times 9 \times 8 \times 7 \times 6 \times 5 \times 4 \times 3 \times 2 \times 1$

patterns – an enormous number which the mathematicians write as 16! and call 'factorial 16'. This is enough variety for a lifetime.

Of course, most of these patterns are abstract and formless; but many resemble faces – faces of people, birds, animals or weird alien beings.

By making in addition to the Transclown tiles a set of fifteen cards (shown opposite), two or more players can compete to make patterns.

Transclown

The sixteen game tiles seen above in the basic face configuration.

Copy, colour and cut out the sixteen tiles along the dissection grid.

Game moves:
1 the basic position
2 horizontal move
3 three possible vertical moves

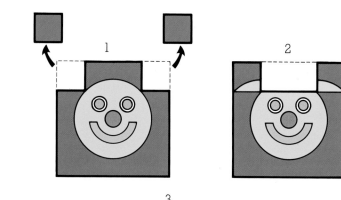

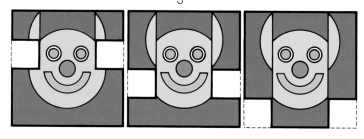

Arrange the sixteen tiles in the standard 'face' position and remove the two top corner pieces.

Shuffle the fifteen cards and place them in a pile, face down. Players take turns to draw three cards from the top of the pile. The players must try to create as many of the faces on his cards as possible by making at most **six** moves with the tiles.

A **move** is made by sliding two tiles into empty spaces, horizontally or vertically. But the moves must be symmetrical about the centre line of the face to preserve the symmetry of the picture. Additionally, in a **vertical** move the tile need not itself move to the empty space; it may instead push any intervening cards into the space.

If any of the faces on the cards is created, that player keeps that card. The rest are returned face down to the bottom of the stack. The game continues until all cards have been taken. The player with the most cards wins.

Many similar games can be devised, made and played.

Transclown game cards

Copy, colour and cut out the set of cards. You can add to the set compositions of your own

Ordinary dominoes are 2 × 1 rectangular tiles with numbered ends, and the standard rules for playing dominoes – adjacent numbers must match – is the best known example of a game using what we have called the domino principle. The rules of dominoes require them to be laid in chains, rather than packed tightly, and commonly the 'doubles' – dominoes with the same number repeated – are laid sideways to the chain: but these are unimportant variations.

Alexander MacMahon (1854–1929) devised a number of generalized domino games, using polygonal dominoes that tile the plane. They are coloured rather than numbered. The sets of tiles are not arbitrary: the same basic shape of tile is coloured in all possible ways to form a complete set of tiles no two of which are alike. (The reflection of a tile is considered to be different, but rotations are considered the same. This is a natural assumption, since the tiles are usually coloured on one side only, so cannot be turned over – but can be rotated in the plane without difficulty.)

The object of the game is to arrange the complete set of tiles, according to the domino principle, in some pleasing and symmetrical pattern.

Several games encountered already fall into the category of generalized dominoes.

There are exactly twenty-four ways to colour the edges of a square with three colours. These possibilities are best represented by dividing the square by diagonals, and colouring each of the four regions so obtained. To each region corresponds exactly one edge.

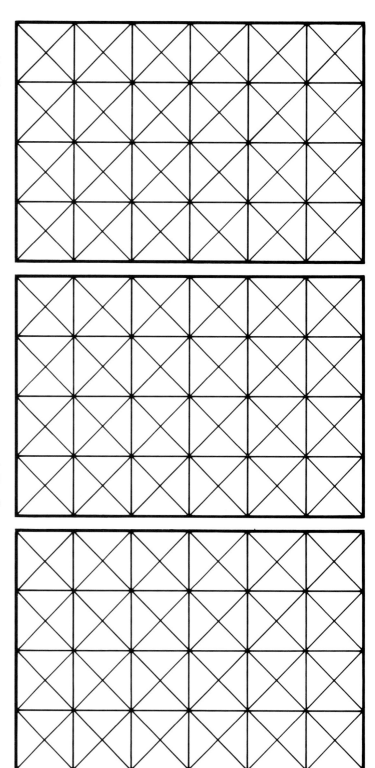

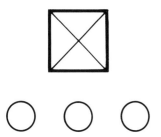

The most symmetrical way to arrange them is in a 4 × 6 rectangle. To make the problem harder, the outer border must be all of one colour.

A complete set of twenty-four triangular tiles may be assembled to form a hexagon. Again, the border should be the same colour all the way round.

Can you find other pleasing arrangements?

MacMahon's mathematical work was based on the theory of symmetric functions – algebraic expressions that remain unchanged if the letters in them are permuted. For example, **a** + **b** + **c** and **ab** + **bc** + **ca** are symmetric functions of **a**, **b** and **c**.

If the colours of a complete set of MacMahon dominoes are permuted, we end up with exactly the same set of tiles as before. The beautiful combinatorial properties of these dominoes derive from this deep permutational symmetry.

Colour squares and triangles of Mac-Mahon

Patterns of a dissected square and triangle are coloured in three and four different colours respectively – creating sets of twenty-four squares and twenty-four triangles. The object is to fit the squares in a 4 × 6 rectangle, and the triangles in a hexagonal configuration, with two conditions:

1 Each pair of touching edges must be of the same colour.

2 The borders of the rectangle and the hexagon must be the same colour all the way round.

There are 12,251 possible solutions; some are shown on pages 116–17

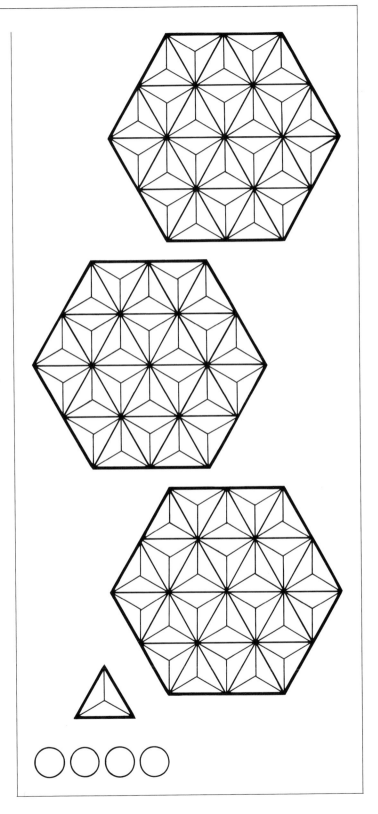

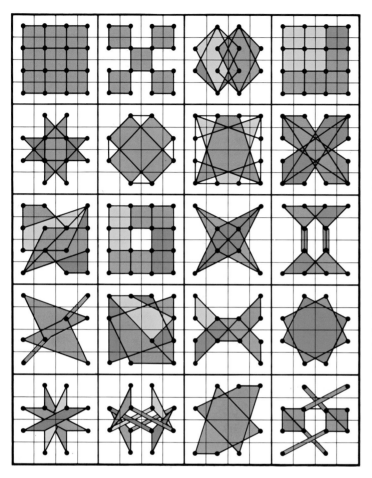

Some of the earliest traces of number speculations can be detected in superstitions concerning numbers. The writing of numbers in patterns started in ancient China, where numbers were **figurate** (i.e. numbers that can form regular patterns, such as squares and triangles, from that many dots) and were represented by lines or circles or dots.

Magic Squares is one of the oldest and most popular puzzles in existence. The first magic square is dated as early as 2200 BC. It was called 'Lo-Shu' and appeared in the Chinese Book of Permutations. The magic square is a set of natural numbers (positive integers) in serial order, beginning with 1, arranged in a square formation, with the following **magic** property: **if you add the numbers in any row, or any column, or either diagonal, you always get the same result.** The **order** of the magic square is the number of cells on one of its sides. There are no magic squares of order 2 and only one of order 3 (the Lo-Shu).

Diabolic magic squares

Albrecht Dürer's etching **Melancholia** includes an order 4 magic square which conceals the date when the etching was created. In Dürer's 'diabolic' magic square shown here, there are many sets of numbers that add up to the magic constant 34. For example, the top 2 × 2 square – 16, 3, 5, 10 – or the central square – 10, 11, 6, 7.

The compositions above are based on such sets of numbers; the patterns are designed to exhibit the geometrical regularities of the sets of numbers involved

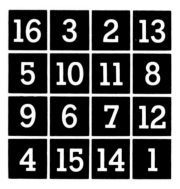

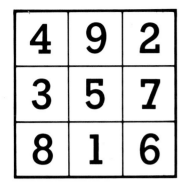

The Lo-Shu magic square

Magic squares grow quickly in number and complexity at the order 4 and higher orders. There are exactly 880 different types of order 4 magic squares, many of which are more 'magic' than required by the magic square.

Leonhard Euler devised a new type of magic square, the Latin square. This is a square in which n symbols are so placed that each row or column contains each symbol exactly once.

Latin square of order 5

Copy and cut out twenty-five square tiles in five colours (five sets of five tiles).

Create first a Latin square of order 5, and then a diagonal Latin square of order 5.

In a two-player game, players alternate by placing tiles on the game board so that no colour appears twice or more times in any direction, horizontally, vertically or diagonally. The winner is the last player able to make a move. Once a tile is placed on the board, it cannot be moved

(Solution: page 116)

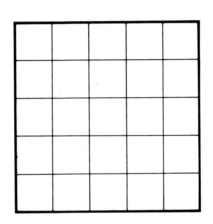

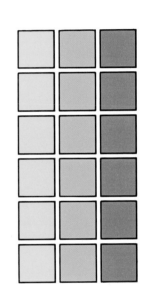

Latin square of order 6

Copy and cut out thirty-six square tiles in six colours (six sets of six tiles).

Create first a Latin square of order 6, and then a diagonal Latin square of order 6. Will the latter be possible? If not, what is the largest number of squares you can place on the board? Can you place thirty-two tiles? In a two-player game, rules as above

(Solution: page 116)

Latin squares are so called because the usual choice of symbols is letters a, b, c, d ... from the Latin alphabet. Suppose a second set of symbols is also chosen: the letters α (alpha), β (beta), γ (gamma), δ (delta) ... of the Greek alphabet. Place one of each type of symbol in each cell of an $n \times n$ square. It is easy enough to arrange that the Latin symbols taken alone form a Latin square, and that the Greek letters alone form a second Latin square. (See the perils of ill-chosen terminology.) To achieve this, merely superimpose two Latin squares, the second translated into Greek.

To produce a creative interaction between the two squares, any pair of symbols should occur once and once only in the combined square. For instance, αβ may occur only once, and so on. Now a random superimposition of Latin squares is probably no longer a solution; repetitions and omissions are common. A solution is called a Graeco-Latin square. (Depending on the size of the square, solutions may or may not be possible.) The two component Latin squares are said to be **orthogonal**.

It is easy to see that no Graeco-Latin square of order 2 can exist. Many other orders can be ruled out by theoretical considerations. Until recently, the order 10 case was an unsolved problem. In 1959 a computer was instructed to search for order 10 Graeco-Latin squares. It searched for 100 hours and found none. Perhaps this was not a total surprise: a complete search would have taken a century.

Nevertheless, the computer's failure appeared to confirm the common view that no such square could exist. However, in 1960 a new method was invented, which produced Graeco-Latin squares of orders 10, 14, 18, etc. For once, sheer brainpower was superior to the computer.

Graeco-Latin squares are not merely a diversion – they have practical uses. Suppose an agricultural scientist wishes to test the effect of fungicides on wheat plants. He has seven types of fungicide to test.

00	47	18	76	29	93	85	34	61	52
86	11	57	28	70	39	94	45	02	63
95	80	22	67	38	71	49	56	13	04
59	96	81	33	07	48	72	60	24	15
73	69	90	82	44	17	58	01	35	26
68	74	09	91	83	55	27	12	46	30
37	08	75	19	92	84	66	23	50	41
14	25	36	40	51	62	03	77	88	99
21	32	43	54	65	06	10	89	97	78
42	53	64	05	16	20	31	98	79	87

Graeco-Latin magic square of order 10

Then he might divide a field into seven parallel strips, running from north to south, and treat each with the fungicide.

However, the conditions that favour fungal growth might vary over the field – possibly from north to south. That experiment would not be conclusive. Strips running east–west would suffer from the same drawback.

If the scientist divides the field into forty-nine plots in a 7×7 matrix, and applies the chemicals according to the prescriptions of a Latin square, all such biases are eliminated. Now suppose that the scientist has not one variety of wheat to test, but seven. Then a Graeco-Latin square

would be appropriate. Euler's recreation is today widely used in the design of experiments in biology, sociology, medicine and even marketing. The 'field' need not, of course, be a piece of land. It might be a cow, a patient, a leaf, a cage of animals, a city, a period of time. The Graeco-Latin square is essentially just a chart of experimental results. Its rows take care of one variable, its columns a second, its Latin symbols a third, its Greek symbols a fourth.

The power of an abstraction lies in its wealth of practical realizations. Many may bear no resemblance to the original motives that led to its invention.

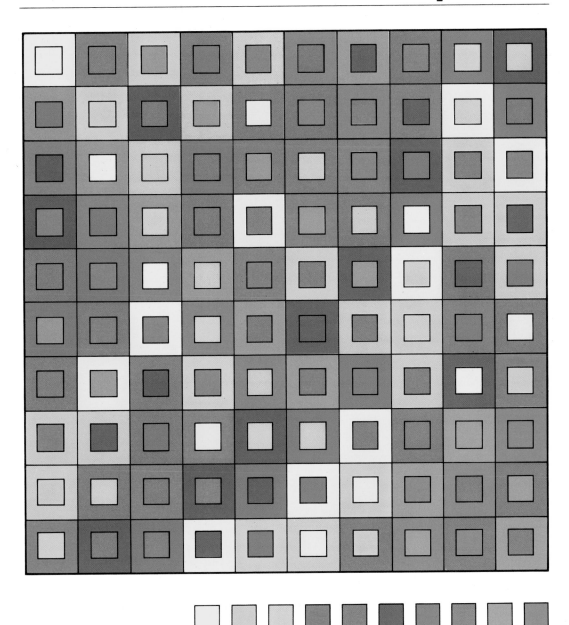

Graeco-Latin magic square of order 10

Colour composition based on the magic square long
thought to be impossible

Given **n** different elements (symbols, colours, people, things), how many different ways can they be arranged in order?

One object, a, can only be arranged in one way.

Two objects, a and b, can be arranged as ab or ba – two ways.

Three objects, a, b and c, can be arranged as – abc, acb, bac, bca, cab, cba – six ways.

Given **n** objects, we may choose the first one in **n** ways. The rest may be arranged in any order we wish. So there are **n** times as many arrangements of **n** things as there are of **n**-1. For example, there are $4 \times 6 = 24$ ways to arrange four things, $5 \times 24 = 120$ ways to arrange five, $6 \times 120 = 720$ ways to arrrange six, and so on. The result, in general, is called **factorial n** and written **n**! It can be calculated by the formula

$$n! = n \times (n\text{-}1) \times (n\text{-}2) \times \ldots 3 \times 2 \times 1.$$

This number becomes very large very rapidly.

The factorial function is the key to many problems about the number of ways to combine things.

The structure of permutations has a deep influence on mathematical thought. For example, there are standard formulae for the solution of equations of the first, second, third and fourth degree. For 400 years no such formula was known for the equation of the fifth degree. Finally Niels Abel and Evariste Galois showed that no such formula could exist. The basic reason? A peculiarity of the permutations of four or fewer symbols (the roots of the equation) that failed to extend to five symbols.

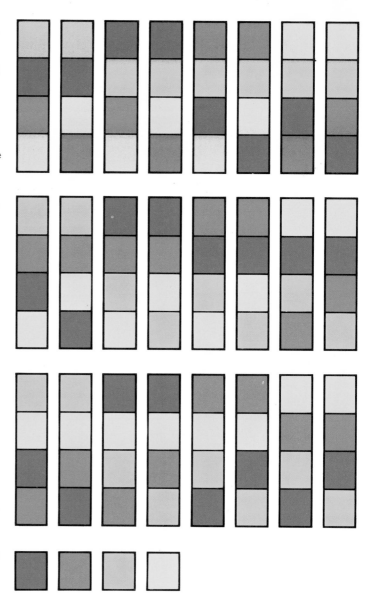

Permutino game

Copy and cut out the twenty-four strips.
Can you form a continuous line of matching colours?

Consider a strip of paper divided into four rectangles. There are 4! = 24 ways to colour this with four colours, using each only once. What is the longest chain you can create, so that adjacent colours are the same?

Can you lay out the strips in a line, each overlapping the previous one by **two** cells, so that colours match on the overlap? Can you make the end similarly match the beginning, so that the snake eats its tail? What about triple overlaps?

If two strips are counted the same if one can be rotated to give the other, how many different ones are there?

Using a 4 × 1 arrangement of squares, make a complete set of twenty-four strips. These can be used to play an enjoyable family game, based once more on the domino principle.

Each player chooses a colour. Deal the strips to players in turn, until all have been dealt. Players take it in turns to add a strip to the pattern on the table. It must match the existing colours along all edges that touch. If a player cannot lay a strip he forfeits his turn. When all strips have been laid, or no player can move, each player finds his score.

Any square belonging to a connected region of squares of his colour that contains **four or more** squares counts as one point. For example, in the sample game blue has seven points because he has a connected region with seven squares in it (and each constitutes one point in the score). In the event of a tie, the player with the largest connected region wins.

Blue won the sample game.

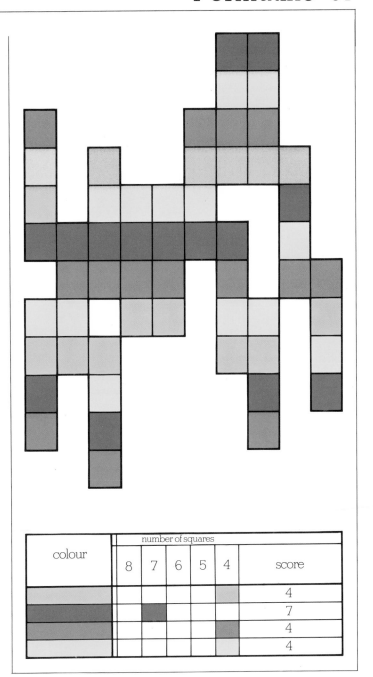

colour	number of squares					score
	8	7	6	5	4	
						4
						7
						4
						4

Permutino game sample
Sample game with its score chart

68 Squaremutation

Divide a square into four fields by its diagonals. There are twenty-four ways to colour such a square using each of four colours once only, provided rotations are considered different. Copy them and cut them out. If patterns differing only by a rotation are considered to be the same, how many different patterns remain? The original twenty-four tiles divide into six groups, each containing the four rotations of a given tile.

To play Squaremutation, make a 5×5 board with squares of the same size. Colour each edge with one of the four colours, and black out the central square to create a hole. Can you place all twenty-four tiles to cover the board, according to the domino principle, so that colours match also at the edges of the board?

For more than one player: lay the tiles face down and mix them. Players take turns to pick one tile and place it on the board so that it touches a previously placed square, and the colours match. The first player unable to place his tile loses the game.

A puzzle: what is the smallest number of tiles needed to block the board, so that no further play is possible with any remaining tile?

The Squaremutation game
The set of twenty-four cyclic permutations

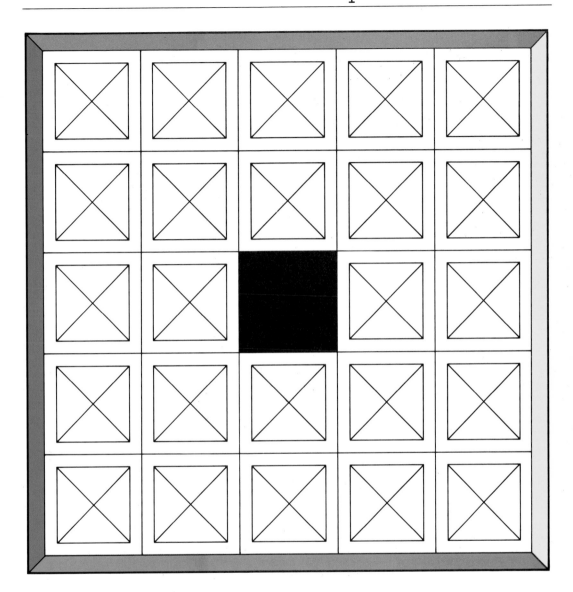

The Squaremutation game board

(Solution: page 116)

Now divide a hexagon into three fields, and use six colours.

Since there are more colours than fields, the number of possible ways to do this is **not** given by a factorial function. It turns out that it is twenty. The board for the game consists of only nineteen hexagonal cells, for reasons of symmetry.

For a single player, the game is a puzzle: place nineteen of the twenty tiles on the board so that the colours match.

For several players, lay the tiles face down and shuffle them. Players take turns to pick a tile and place it anywhere on the board. However, in this game new tiles are not required to be adjacent to an existing tile. Nevertheless the colours must match if it **is** adjacent. Anyone who cannot play drops out of the game (replacing the unplayed tile face down, which must be mixed with the others on the table). The winner is the last player left in the game.

The Hexatile
game set

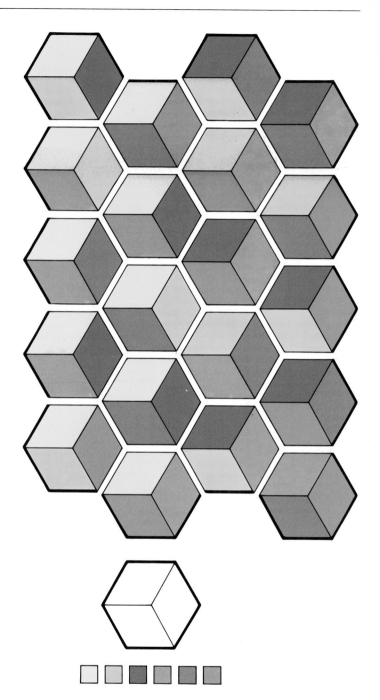

The Hexatile game board

(Solution: page 117)

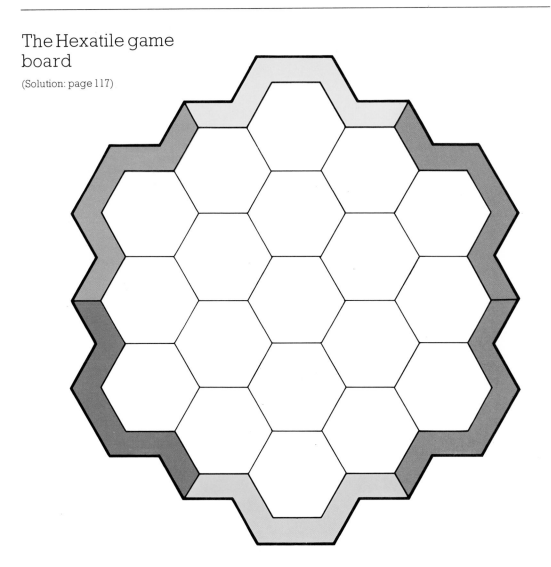

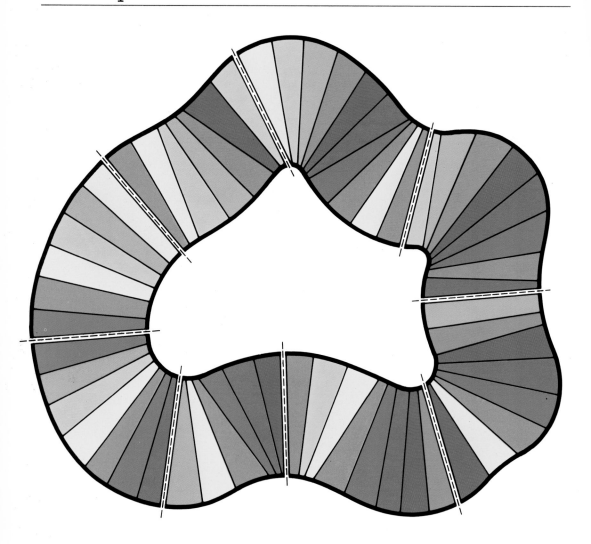

Serpent game

Copy this puzzle and cut it along the outer and inner
contours. Then divide it into eight pieces by cutting along
the dashed lines.
Shuffle the parts.
Now try to reassemble them into the original closed
serpentine shape – without looking at the book.
You will get lots of serpents, but it's a lot harder to make the
snake eat its tail. Trial and error takes a long time, so a little
thought is in order.
A hint: each of its parts contains the key to the solution

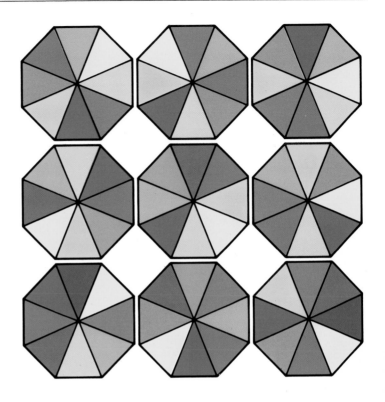

Octopuz game

Copy and cut out the nine octagons. Rearrange them in the original 3 × 3 configuration so that edges that touch have the same colour.

(Solution: page 117)

Did you ever wonder how many ways there are for two eight-tentacled octopi to 'shake tentacles'? If you number the tentacles from 1 to 8, then the 'tentacle-shake' determines (and is determined by) a permutation of those numbers.
So the answer is 8! = 40,320.
This shows how easy the solution to the Octopuz puzzle is: all you have to do is find the **right** arrangement.

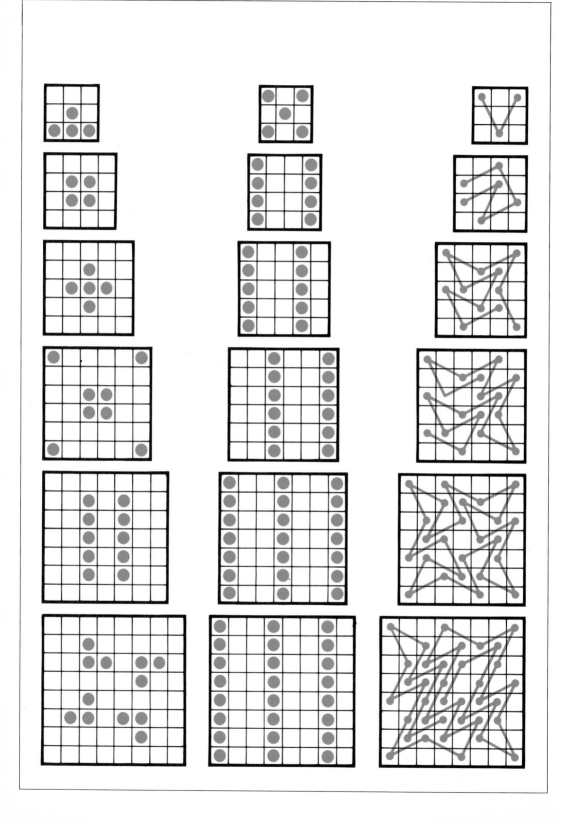

These are not **chess** problems – that is, they are not portions of real games of chess. They are problems based on the chess pieces and the chessboard.

Knight's problems (on page 74)

THE MINIMAL KNIGHT'S PROBLEM

What is the smallest number of knights that can be placed on a square board so that all unoccupied cells are under attack by at least one knight? The left-hand column of the picture shows solutions for 3-sided to 8-sided boards.

THE MAXIMAL KNIGHT'S PROBLEM

What is the largest number of knights that can be placed on a board so that no two attack each other? (Second column in picture.)

THE UNCROSSED KNIGHT'S TOUR

How far can the knight get without crossing his tracks? (Third column in picture.)

1 Rook's tour

The rook moves horizontally or vertically, as far as he likes.
Find as many rook's tours as you can.
How many different paths are possible altogether?
What is the smallest number of moves that the rook can make a tour in? A thirty-move tour is shown.

2 Bishop's tour

The bishop moves diagonally, so His Grace is confined to the squares of a single colour. He may move as far as he wishes, in a straight line, at each move.
Find the bishop's tours.
How many paths are there?
What is the smallest number of moves possible?

3 Queen's tour

Her Majesty the Queen combines the powers of both rook and bishop (the Military and the Church). Move the queen so that she visits all the squares of the board in fourteen moves. She must finish on the square that she started from. Squares may be visited **more than once if necessary**.

1 ▽

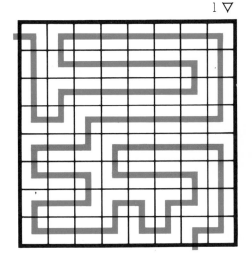

2 ▽

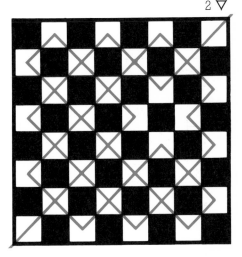

3 ▽

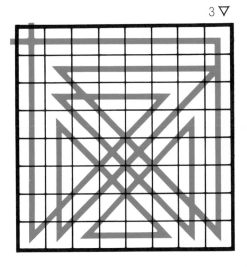

Knight's tour

Remember how a chess knight moves? He can go to any space that is distant two squares horizontally and one vertically, or two vertically and one horizontally.

One of the oldest and most interesting of chessboard puzzles is the Knight's Tour. Can the knight be made to visit every square of the board exactly once, by a series of legal moves? The size of the board need not be the usual 8×8 chessboard.

Mathematically, this is a question about graphs. Think of the squares on the board as nodes; and join the nodes by an edge if there is a legal knight's move that connects them. (That is, squares are not connected

Knight's tours

Original compositions based on 'magic lines' of knight's tours by adjacency in the ordinary sense, but in 'knight space'.)

Does there exist a Hamiltonian Path? The tour is **closed** if the knight returns to his original home on the final move. Closed tours can only occur on even-sided boards. To see this, note that the knight changes the colour of his square on each move, if the squares are in the usual chequered pattern. On an odd-sided board he makes an even number of moves, so must end on the same colour square; the final leap home would thus end on the wrong colour and so cannot exist. On the usual chessboard there are at least several million different knight's tours. Euler found many with unusual symmetries. Here we show some original designs based on knight's tours.

Given a chessboard of order **n**, how many queens can be placed on it so that no queen attacks another? Equivalently, how many counters can you place on the board so that no two lie in the same row, column, or diagonal?

With a 4 × 4 board, there is room for four queens to live in peace and harmony. See how well you can do for other sizes.

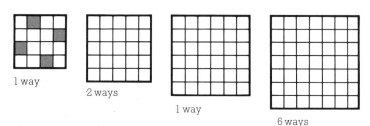

1 way

2 ways

1 way

6 ways

Chessboard standoff

For boards of order 4, 5, 6 and 7

Chessboard queen problem

For an 8 × 8 board there are twelve different solutions

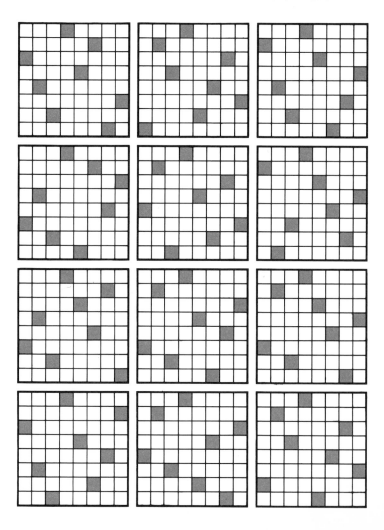

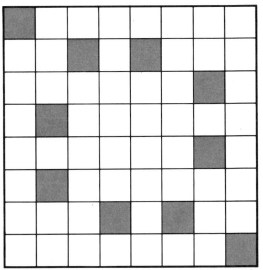

n = 1

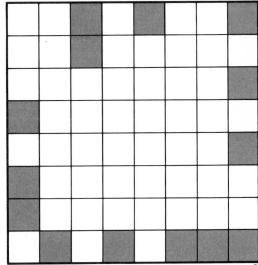

n = 2

Generalized chessboard queen standoff

Choose a number; call it **n**.
What is the largest number of queens that can be placed on an ordinary (8×8) chessboard so that each queen attacks exactly **n** others?
For **n** = 1, the number of queens is ten and there are twelve different solutions.
The best result to date for **n** = 3 is the ridiculously simple one shown. Even if this **is** the answer, it seems less than ridiculously simple to demonstrate the fact.
For **n** = 4, the best result known is 220 queens.
Can you place twenty queens on a chessboard so that each attacks exactly four other queens?
For **n** larger than four, **no solutions can exist**. This is true no matter how large the chessboard may be. (Can you prove it? What about an infinite board?)

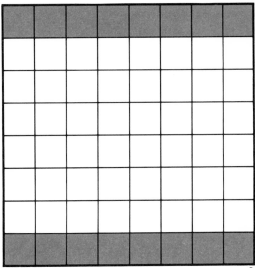

n = 3

Copy and cut out the square tiles with their radiating lines. Each side is coloured with four different colours.

Arrange all sixteen squares in a 4 × 4 array, obeying the domino principle.

Don't use trial and error: think. There's a logical shortcut

(Solution: page 118)

Copy and cut out the four squares shown. This time, each side is coloured in six different colours.

For exactly one of the colours, it is not possible to form a continuous zigzag line through a stack of the four squares. Which colour is the odd one out?

You have precisely one minute to solve this problem, starting ... now

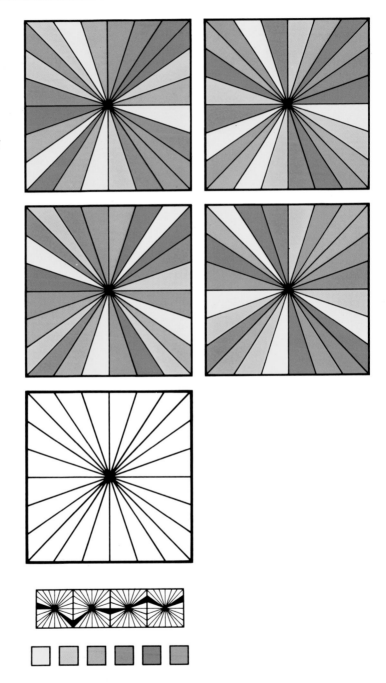

82 Venerable beads

A necklace has **n** beads. Some are red, the rest yellow. How many different necklaces are there? Try **n** = 1, 2, 3, 4, 5, 6 and 7. Rotations and reflections should **not** be counted as different for this problem.

The solutions for the first six values of **n** are shown, and the table below gives the number of solutions for **n** up to 20.

No. BEADS	No. NECKLACES
1	2
2	3
3	4
4	6
5	8
6	13
7	18
8	30
9	46
10	78
11	125
12	224
13	380
14	687
15	1224
16	2250
17	4112
18	7685
19	14,310
20	27,012

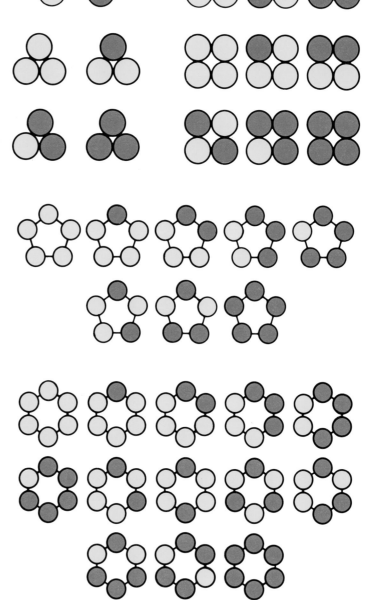

The necklace-colouring problem

Solutions for 1 to 6 beads

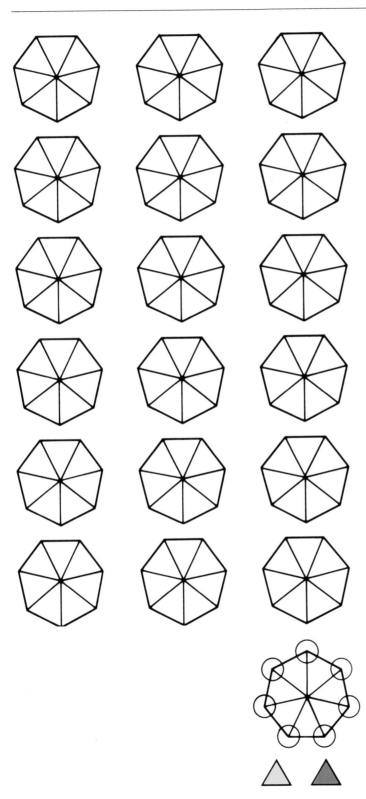

There is an equivalent geometric problem about polygons. For example, let $n = 7$. How many ways are there to colour a heptagon (a seven-sided regular polygon) using two colours?

The problem would be very easy to solve if rotations and reflections were not allowed. With them, it becomes distinctly tricky.

In the language of information theory, there is an equivalent problem: how many binary-code words (sequences of 0s and 1s) are there of a given length, ruling out as identical those words that have the same sequence of digits in cyclic order, either clockwise or anti-clockwise?

One way to approach the problem is by using the mathematical theory of symmetry groups. But that's another story.

The necklace-colouring problem for seven beads

Find and colour all the eighteen different two-colour necklaces consisting of seven beads. Then copy and cut out the coloured septagons and try to create a colour-matching configuration of them all

(Solution: page 119)

This is the most complex of our collection of combinatorial domino problems. Copy and cut out twenty-five tiles like the one shown, and colour them according to the illustration. Now rearrange them in a 5×5 square, to conform with the domino principle (colours must match).

The number of possible configurations is

$$2^{25} \times 25!$$

which is **enormous**.

One of them is right. Which? By arranging the twenty-five tiles **without** conforming to the domino condition, innumerable patterns may be formed, including many that are pleasing to the eye. The four compositions illustrated here form a sequence in which the degree of order present in the pattern becomes less and less. It is hard to believe that all these compositions are made up from the same basic elements.

When you find the solution it will look altogether different again. When a solid melts, or a liquid boils, the atoms that make it up reform themselves into systems having less internal order. Such events are called **phase transitions**. We see that phase transitions may occur in art as well as in nature.

The order imposed by the domino principle produces new effects. Matching colours lead to merging patterns. The figure-ground optical illusion and visual reversal add a dynamic dimension.

Is the solution to the puzzle also the most pleasing of the compositions? If you think it is, does this prove the necessity of design, which is a plan for order?

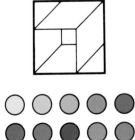

The universe that we inhabit is vast, the laws of nature complex and inscrutable. But even a simple universe, with simple laws, holds many surprises.

Modern computers operate like small universes. The laws of nature are the programs that control what they do. Even a simple program can produce a rich variety of results. One of the fathers of the modern computer, John von Neumann, developed a theory of **cellular automata**: basically, simple computers stripped down to their mathematical essentials. A cellular automaton consists of a lot of square cells. At each instant in time, the state of a given cell changes according to the states of the neighbouring cells.

Despite their simplicity, cellular automata behave in surprising ways. For example, it is possible to choose the rules by which cells influence each other in such a way that a self-reproducing configuration of states exists. That is, we can build a 'creature' capable of reproducing itself. Indeed, in its fundamental components, this 'creature' resembles a living being, and reproduces according to the same kind of 'genetic' scheme.

We can explore cellular automata by drawing blobs, or moving counters, on a square grid. The rules are given below. Choose your 'creature' – some starting configuration of blobs – and watch it grow.

The allowed states of cells are:
[a] empty
[b] red
[c] black

The creature evolves, move by move, according to the following laws:

[a] An empty square which adjoins one (and only one) red or black square becomes black (this represents a 'birth').

[b] All new black squares appear simultaneously on a given move.

[c] All previously black squares become red ('ageing').

[d] All previously red squares become empty ('death').

You can use counters on a board to follow the successive generations of any creature you choose. Variations on the rules are possible. A famous set of rules was devised by John Horton Conway. He calls the resulting system 'Life'. Physicists use similar ideas to study how solids turn to liquids, or liquids to gases. They call them 'lattice dynamics'.

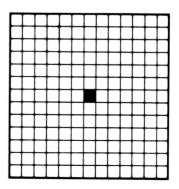

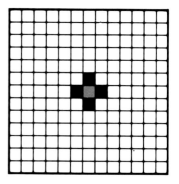

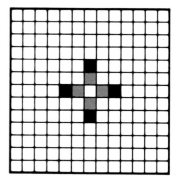

Growth pattern of a square matrix
The first nine generations. Continue the pattern for further generations

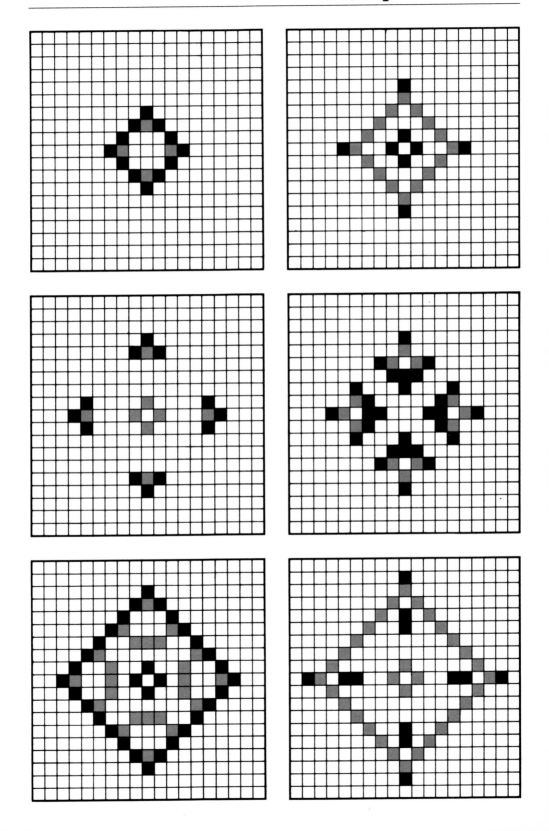

There are many variations on the 'growth pattern' idea. They are being studied more frequently because of their applications to physics, crystallography, computer science and biology. The spread of infection through a forest of trees, or through a tissue made up of cells, can be modelled in this way. Models based on square cells, or triangular cells, are especially suited to computer calculations. In fact, in a sense, almost everything done on a computer is a kind of cellular growth pattern.

For example, consider weather prediction. The computer divides the earth's atmosphere into thousands of cells. From the state of a cell **today** (temperature, pressure, humidity, etc.) it derives the state **tomorrow** by making a whole series of 'moves' on a very short timescale. The traditional weather map is assembled from the information in the cells.

Crystals grow according to simple geometric principles: their atoms are stacked according to a regular lattice structure. The remarkable diversity of crystal forms shows how much freedom is left by the underlying regularity. No two snow crystals are alike.

Biological growth is an ever present puzzle. An early study was made by D'Arcy Thompson in his famous book **On Growth and Form**. He noted a systematic type of growth in living organisms. Molluscs secrete their protective shells by a process of continuing expansion. Each added section of shell is similar to, but larger than, its predecessor. The beautiful spirals of many shells derive from this simple principle. So do the patterns of sunflower seeds. There is immense freedom for the creative exploitation of growth patterns, especially in art and music. The solutions to the growth patterns included here show a few examples, but they represent only the tip of an iceberg.

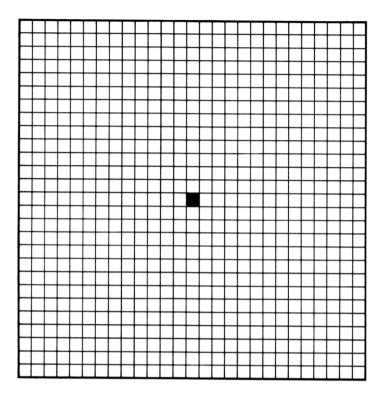

Growth pattern of squares – thirteen generations

In the first generation there is a single square, at the centre. Additional squares are supplied at each new generation, subject to the single law: no square may be added which touches two sides of the former generation's squares. For vividness, each generation should be painted in a different colour.

Try to complete the pattern up to the thirteenth generation.

How many squares are there in each generation?

What number sequence do they represent?

Are there any regularities in the pattern?

Could the pattern become indefinitely large?

Try the above rules with the pattern of triangles and compare the two solutions.

These are just some of the intriguing questions that such patterns raise. Devise your own growth laws and see what your patterns do.

Ask – and answer – the same questions.

For example, try this law: no new square may touch any member of previous generations. What happens now?

(Solution: page 120)

colour	☐		△
1			
2			
3			
4			
5			
6			
7			
8			
9			
10			
11			
12			
13			

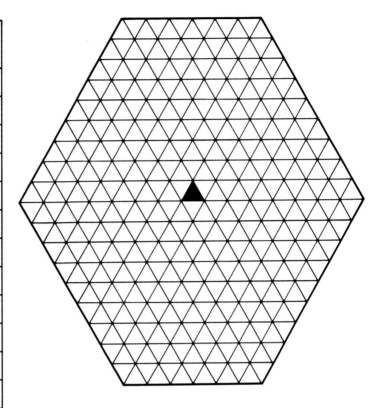

Growth pattern of triangles

The idea of growth patterns may be explored on other kinds of grid, in particular a grid of triangles. Depending on the choice of growth rules, different sequences of patterns will be generated.

Sample rules:

[a] No new triangle may touch more than two previous triangles

[b] Each new triangle must touch an odd number of old triangles

[c] If an old triangle is touched by two others, a new triangle may not be added so as to touch it

[d] At each stage, every old triangle 'gives birth' to three adjacent triangles (along its edges) and then 'dies'

[e] At each stage, every old triangle gives birth to twelve new triangles (all those that touch it at edges or corners) and then 'dies'

Experiment with these and other rules; see what kinds of patterns you obtain

(Solution: page 120)

Labelled Plates

If we have five plates, which are 'labelled' by being coloured in five different colours, and five objects, how many ways are there to distribute the objects so that each plate holds **one** object?

A moment's thought shows that this is just another way of asking in how many different ways can the five objects be arranged in order (assign numbers 1–5 to the colours and use these to define the order). So the answer is just the number of permutations of five things, that is, $5! = 120$.

But we can change the rules. Suppose we allow any number of objects, from zero to five, on any plate. How many different ways can they be placed?

One object, one plate: one way. This is trivial!

It's not hard to see that two objects may be placed on two plates in four ways. Before reading on, try to list all the possibilities for three objects on three plates.

The answer is 27. Did you find them all?

Let's think about those numbers. We have:

$1 = 1^1$ way to place 1 object on 1 plate

$4 = 2^2$ ways to place 2 objects on 2 plates

$27 = 3^3$ ways to place 3 objects on 3 plates....

This might just be coincidence; but a good guess is that there will be **n** ways to place **n** objects on **n** plates.

That is, $4^4 = 256$ ways for four objects on four plates; and $5^5 = 3125$ for five.

In fact this guess is the correct answer. It was proved by the famous mathematician Arthur Cayley. It can be proved using ideas about tree graphs. Plates and trees are sisters under the skin, like the Colonel's Lady and Judy O'Grady (or so says Rudyard Kipling).

Unlabelled Plates

Suppose instead that all the plates are the same colour – unlabelled plates. And suppose there is no way to tell which plate is which. What is the pattern of numbers?

Try to work out the number of ways to place **n** objects on **n** unlabelled plates when **n** is 1, 2, 3.

This is a real-life problem. Suppose we wish to place a husband and wife in two beds. There are two essentially different ways: both in the same bed, or one in each. Most people would agree that it doesn't matter much which bed is which. So for $n = 2$ the answer is 2.

There are five ways to put three people into three beds (i.e. three objects on three unlabelled plates). Or, in a less risqué interpretation, consider alliances between three nations. There are five ways to form an alliance between them.

Anyway, back to the puzzle. There are fifteen ways for $n = 4$ and fifty-two when $n = 5$. The pattern in the numbers is certainly more elusive than plain old n^n.

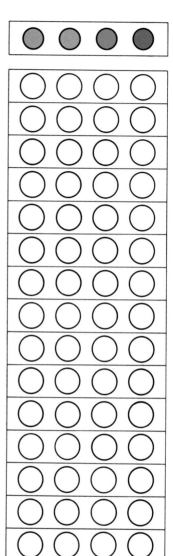

Two objects on two plates

Using two colours, there are four ways to distribute two objects on two plates

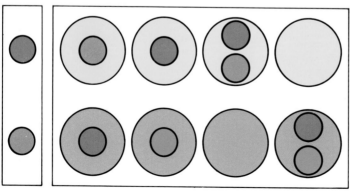

Four objects on four unlabelled plates

Using four colours, draw in the different ways

Three objects on three plates ▷

Using three colours, draw in all the different ways in which three objects can be distributed on three plates

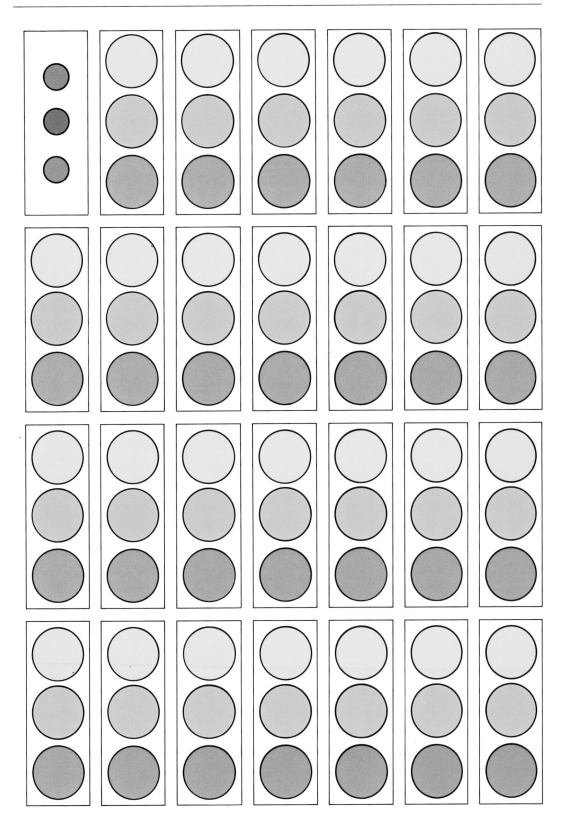

92 Persistence

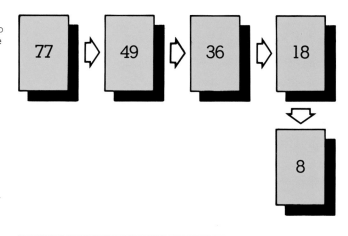

Think of a number . . .
It's a standard enough beginning to a variety of number tricks. But we're going to give it a new twist. Let's suppose the number was 723. Multiply the digits together. This gives $7 \times 2 \times 3 = 42$. Repeat the process ($4 \times 2 = 8$). Repeat again ($8 = 8$). We're stuck. The whole series of calculations stops after three steps. In recreational number theory, we say that the **persistence** of the original number, 723, is 3.

In general, the persistence of a number is the number of stages required to reduce it to a single digit by repeatedly multiplying all its digits together.

For example, the persistence of 77 is found by repeated multiplications: $77 \rightarrow 49 \rightarrow 36 \rightarrow 18 \rightarrow 8$, so is 4.

Here are some more problems:
[a] What is the smallest number of persistence 1? (Easy!)
[b] What are the smallest numbers of persistence 2, 3, 4, 5?
[c] Does 'persistence' always make sense? That is, must every starting number lead to a single-digit number in the end? Or can the process go on for ever?

The persistence concept can be used to define a variety of games, whose object is to give practice in multiplication. The basic materials for the game will be a set of cards: single-digit numbers, together with all two-digit numbers that can occur as products.

In fact, since 9 can only be produced from 33 and 33 won't be produced from any two-digit number, we leave these out too. So we can now select sixty-four different numbers: 0 1 2 3 4 5 6 7 8 10 12 14 15 16 18 20 21 24 25 27 28 30 32 35 36 39 40 41 42 43 44 45 46 47 48 49 50 51 52 53 54 55 56 57 58 59 60 61 62 63 64 65 66 67 68 69 70 71 72 73 74 75 76 77 88

These are the cards. Your job is to invent the games. For example, players could take turns adding cards to an array in which each new card must be adjacent to one that forms the next stage in the persistence calculation; that is, the product of the digits of the new card must equal the value of the card it is placed next to. Or players could be asked to add cards to a sequence, obeying the same rule.

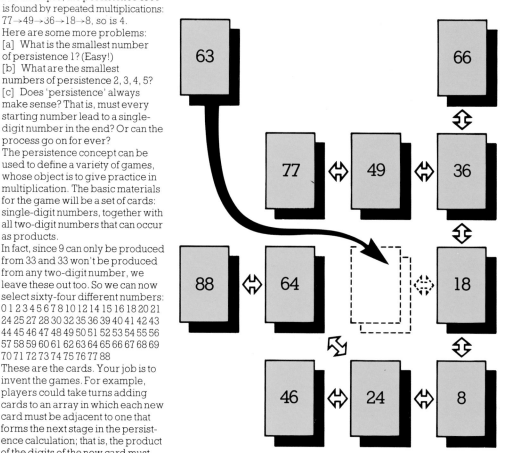

Persisto game

Top: a Persisto sequence.
Bottom: a Persisto solitaire configuration (i.e. a game played by one player using Persisto sequences)

Copy and cut out the sixteen coloured squares on the right. The object of the game is to place all sixteen squares on the game board one at a time, obeying the following rules:

[a] Do not place a piece on a square of the same colour, or next to a square of the same colour ('next to' includes squares that are adjacent diagonally).

[b] After each move, a square on the board assumes the colour of the piece that covers it, so far as rule [a] is concerned on subsequent moves.

This game can be played by one player, or competitively by two. Two players alternate, adding a piece according to the rules; the first unable to play loses.

(Solution: page 121)

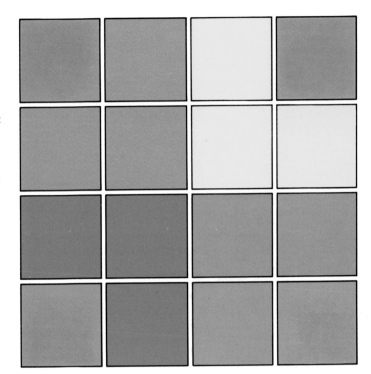

Spectrix game board

For more than two thousand years the geometry of Euclid was generally considered to be the only possible geometry – a 'self-evident truth' which, like so many fondly held beliefs, eventually turned out not only not to be self-evident, but not even true. (To claim that something is 'self-evident' is an excuse, not a proof; it means that nobody has any real idea **why** it is true.) Less than two centuries ago, a number of non-Euclidean geometries were developed which were just as valid as Euclid's geometry.

Non-Euclidean geometries differ from Euclid's in various ways; a basic reason for looking for them was to find geometries in which Euclid's axiom of parallels is not true. That is, to find consistent geometries in which all lines meet (so there are no parallels) or in which there are many parallels to a given line through a given point. These geometries may seem strange at first, but they have important applications, especially in cosmology and modern physics; and they are still the subject of much research.

The most important non-Euclidean geometries are not very easy to describe, however. A more approachable geometry is Taxicab Geometry, which you can explore

Taxicab geometry
Circles of radii 1, 2, 3, 4, 5 and 6

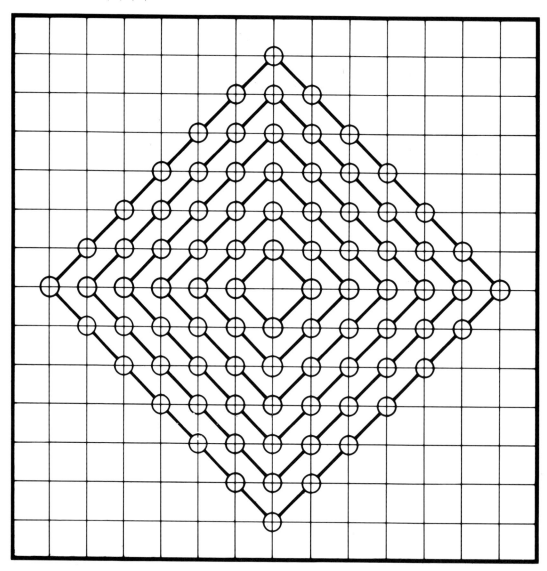

with ease on ordinary graph paper. Imagine a modern city in which streets run on a square grid: north–south or east–west. If you must travel by taxicab, you should measure distances not 'as the crow flies', but 'as the cab drives' – that is, along the lines of the grid. Taxicab distances are in general longer than ordinary distances, except along straight tracks.

Let's consider taxicab circles. In ordinary geometry, a circle consists of all points a fixed distance from the centre. It is, of course, circular in shape. In taxicab geometry we use the same definition but the shape changes....

For example, suppose you live in a city which has six blocks to the kilometre and you travel by a taxi a distance of 1 kilometre. Where can you get to?

You could go six blocks east; or five east and one north; or four east and two north ... and so on. These points lie on the 'taxicab circle' of 'radius' 1 kilometre. But if you draw them on graph paper you'll see you get a **square**.

So in taxicab geometry, circles are squares, and many of Euclid's axioms (geometrical laws) no longer hold. For example, in Euclidean geometry there is always exactly one shortest path between two points. In taxicab geometry there will be a shortest path; but there may be several paths of exactly the same 'shortest' distance.

Of course, some Euclidean properties still hold too. You can explore taxicab geometry by trying to decide which do and which don't. For example, in Euclidean geometry, any two different circles can have at most two points in common. Is this true for taxicab geometry? Be careful.

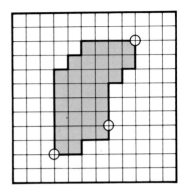

A taxicab scalene triangle

A triangle of sides 14, 8 and 6.

Can you have other triangles of the same sides?

Taxicab squares of side 6

How many squares of the same side are there?

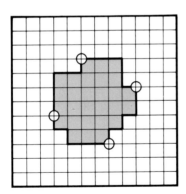

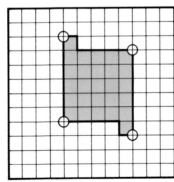

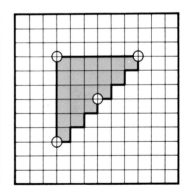

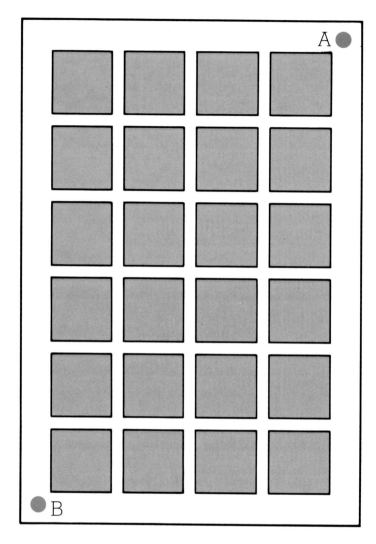

A ●

● B

Minimal route problem

A man who lives at the top right corner works in an office at the bottom left.

The shortest path is ten blocks long.

How many different routes are there connecting the two spots?

The famous Pascal's triangle can easily solve such problems

Let's take a closer look at the reason why there may be more than one shortest route between two points. In fact, let's work out how many such routes there will be.

It helps to tilt the grid 45° and to look at one quarter of it. This gives a triangle. The point at the top is 'home'. There's only one way to stay home, so we put a 1 in that position. There is exactly one way to go to each of the points in the next layer down; mark 1s in those too.

Now consider the third layer. The only way to get to its left-hand end is via the end of the layer above. But the middle position can be reached in two ways: either via the position above and to the left, or above and to the right. Then there's only one way to reach the right-hand end. So place the numbers 1, 2, 1 on the diagram.

In general, to get to a given position:

[a] if it is on the end of a layer, there is only one way;

[b] if not, there are two points above it: one to the left, the other to the right. If these can be reached in m and n ways respectively, then the point below them can be reached in $m + n$ ways.

So we can extend the numbering by using the rules:

[a] place 1s at the ends of layers;

[b] make each number other than those at the end equal to the sum of the numbers immediately above and to the left or right.

So the next layer goes

1 (end of layer)
3 $(1 + 2)$
3 $(2 + 1)$
1 (end of layer)

The next goes

1 (end of layer)
4 $(1 + 3)$
6 $(3 + 3)$
4 $(3 + 1)$
1 (end of layer)

and so on.

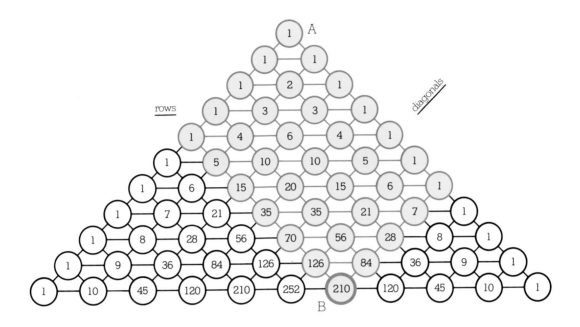

Pascal's Triangle

The resulting numbered triangle is called **Pascal's Triangle**, after its inventor Blaise Pascal.
There is also a formula in terms of factorials for the number in the $(s + 1)$th position along the $(r + 1)$th layer, namely

$$\frac{r!}{s! \, (r-s)!}$$

For example, the third position along the fifth layer holds the numbers

$$\frac{4!}{2! \, (4-2)!} = \frac{24}{2 \times 2} = 6$$

since $2! = 2 \times 1 = 2$.

The formula was known to Isaac Newton, and is involved in his famous Binomial Theorem. The above formula is often shortened to the symbol

$$\binom{r}{s}$$

Among other things, this gives the number of different ways to choose **s** things from among a total of **r**.

In Pascal's Triangle each number is the sum of the two numbers above it.
The lowest corner of the A–B rectangle inserted in Pascal's Triangle marks the answer: there are 210 distinct paths between A and B.
A simple factorial formula can also give the answer:

$$\frac{n!}{a! \, b!} = \frac{10!}{6! \times 4!} = 210$$

You can even see this for the taxicab distance problem. To get to layer 5, say, you must make four moves. To get to the third position along, exactly **two** of those moves must be to the right. So you must choose two moves out of four. This can be done in $\binom{4}{2}$ ways, that is 6, as before. So here there is a connection between taxicab geometry and combinatorial formulae.

The ancient Greeks allowed only straight lines and circles in their geometry. But with a little imagination, even these simple elements can be used to create beautiful and unusual designs.

Draw a circle, and divide its circumference into thirty-six equal parts at 10° intervals with a protractor. Draw in a diameter of the circle, that is, a line joining one of these marked points to the point exactly opposite.

You are now going to draw a kind of spider's web, by moving this diameter. Move the top end one mark clockwise; but move the bottom end **two** marks clockwise. Join these marks. Now repeat, and continue until you get back to where you started from, always moving one end one mark and the other two. We might call this a '1:2 web', although it has a grander name: the **cardioid** or heart curve.

By changing the step sizes 1 and 2 to **m** and **n** we get an **m:n** web. The 1:3 web is called a **nephroid** or kidney curve; and the 2:3 web is the **ranunculoid** or buttercup curve. Each curve shows up clearly, even though it is not actually made up from parts of the lines; it is the **envelope** of the web of lines, and each line in the web is tangent to this envelope.

Try other values for **m** and **n**, for example, 1:4 and 2:5. All of these curves are examples of **epicycloids**.

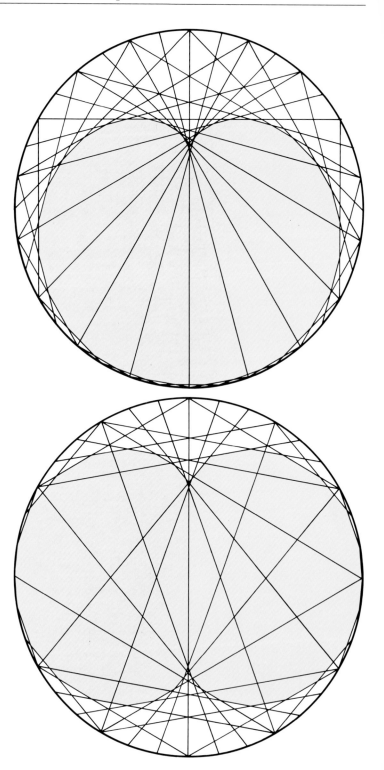

If the spider is drunk, he will weave in circles instead of straight lines. This leads to new possibilities for designs.

For example, draw a single fixed circle, the **base circle**, and choose a point, the **base point**. Draw lots of circles whose centres lie on the base circle and which pass through the base point. For neat designs, divide the base circle into equal segments (say at 10° intervals) and place the compass point in turn on these divisions, opening it just wide enough to reach to the base point.

The curves you now obtain as envelopes are examples of **limaçons**. Different choices of base points give different shapes.

Try a base point that lies on the base circle. Do you recognize the curve? It's a cardioid again.

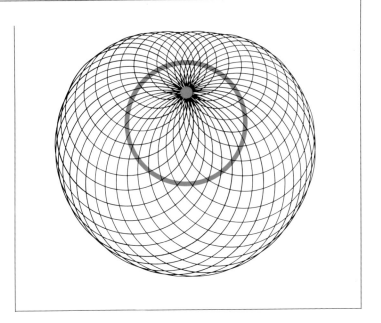

Curves from circles

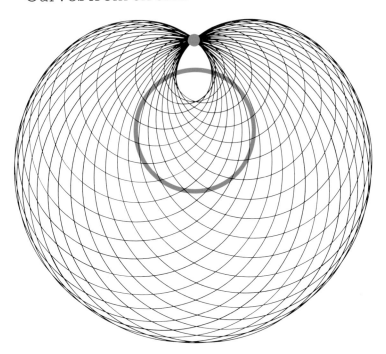

Topology is the study of continuity. A **topological invariant** of shape is a property that is unchanged by any continuous deformation; the shape can be bent, twisted, stretched and compressed – what stays the same? Not much at first sight. The size, the angles, the area – all these can be changed. The typical topological invariant is the hole in a doughnut. Even a bent doughnut still has a hole. The subtlety of topological ideas emerges if we remark that the hole is not, in fact, a **part** of the doughnut at all. ... Topology is sometimes called 'rubber sheet geometry'. To a topologist, a doughnut and a coffee cup are the same: each has a hole. (The coffee cup hole is in the handle; the place you put the coffee is just a dent and doesn't go all the way through. You could flatten it out continuously to get a plate with a handle, but it wouldn't be much good for holding coffee.)

Put in this way, topology sounds, at best, whimsical, though probably entertaining enough. It is not. It is absolutely fundamental. The whole of mathematics is pervaded by ideas of continuity, and so is much applied science. During the last fifty years topology has become a very powerful branch of mathematics and during the last decade it has made a considerable impact in important applications to physics, chemistry and biology.

At that level, topology is neither whimsical nor (except to experts) entertaining. But some of its basic concepts can be grasped by playing games based on topological invariance.

Given some shapes, which of them are topologically the same, and which are not?

Topological equivalence

In each drawing the top figure is deformed into one of the three configurations below it.

Which is the deformed figure?

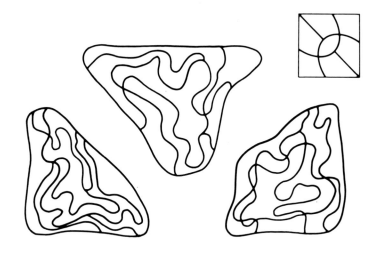

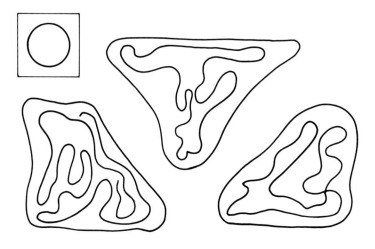

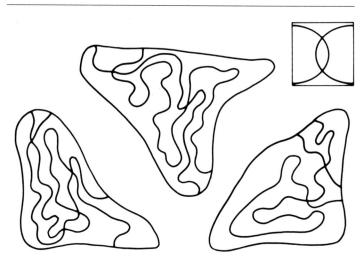

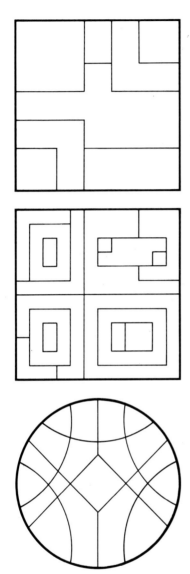

The colour theories of topology

What is the minimum number of colours needed to colour these maps so that no two regions with a common border will have the same colour?

(Solution: page 121)

Until recently this was the **four-colour problem**. Simple enough to state: how many colours are needed so that any map in the plane can be coloured in such a way that no two adjacent regions have the same colour? Simple enough to guess the answer too: **four**. (Adjacent regions must touch along part of an edge, not just at single points.)

What about proofs? It's not hard to show that at least four colours are needed. A mathematician called Kempe published a proof that no map needed five colours. A decade later it was noticed that he had made a subtle mistake, and that the best his proof would show was that no map required **six**. That left a tantalizing gap.

For about a century, people wrestled with the problem. Nobody could find a map needing five colours and nobody could show that no such map existed. The problem acquired some notoriety as one of the simplest unsolved problems to state, and one of the hardest to solve. To make things worse, analogous problems posed on more complicated surfaces could be answered completely. For example, a map on a doughnut can always be coloured with seven colours; and there exist maps for which six colours do **not** work. So seven is the exact number needed in general. On a strange one-sided surface called a **Klein Bottle**, six colours are both necessary and sufficient.

In a sense, the four-colour problem is a bit of a curiosity. Although it seems extremely hard to solve, it is a little offbeat compared with the main concerns of topologists. In a sense, it really doesn't **matter** whether the answer is four or five. On the other hand, it's frustrating not to be able to decide it.

In the late 1970s, two mathematicians at the University of Illinois made a sustained attempt at the problem. For over four years they experimented on a computer, trying to understand what characteristics would make a map four-colourable. Kenneth Appel and Wolfgang Haken eventually came up with a list of 1936 special maps. These formed an 'unavoidable set', which meant that every map must contain at least one of them somewhere inside it. They also evolved a technique called **reducibility**. If a map contains a reducible submap (i.e. a smaller map to which the reducibility technique can be applied), then it is four-colourable. And they found they could solve the four-colour problem if it could be shown that each of their 1936 special maps was reducible.

Not only that: it was possible to pose this question in a form that was suited to computer calculations. If the computer said yes, the problem was solved. (If it said no, incidentally, that would just show that the set of 1936 maps wasn't the right one to use; it wouldn't **disprove** the result.) The computer program ran for 1200 hours on a fast machine; and after some ten billion calculations.... 'Yes!'

So now it's the **Four-Colour Theorem**.

More interesting than the answer is the way it was found. There are good reasons to think that nothing much shorter than the 1200-hour computer calculation will ever be found. If so, there are simple and true theorems which have immensely long and complicated proofs.

There are exactly five different regular solids (polyhedra) shown in the picture. You can think of each polyhedron as a map on a sphere. (It's a rather bent and bumpy sphere, but to topologists none of that matters.) How many colours are needed to colour each map? By the general theorem we know that at most four are; but maybe in these special examples fewer colours suffice.

It's hard to think sensibly about the problem by drawing pictures of the solids, because the front obscures what's going on at the back. Instead, we make a small hole in the middle of one region (this is **not** a topological deformation, but it clearly makes no difference to the number of colours), and then we stretch the punctured sphere open into a disc (which **is** a topological deformation). Now we have to colour the regions formed by the **graph** of the polyhedron – the network formed by its edges. So there's a connection between graphs, maps and topology. One minor point to notice: these maps have a single **infinite** region completely surrounding them. Colour this first. If you forget, you'll think that the tetrahedron can be coloured with three colours, which isn't true: it definitely needs four, because each region touches the other three, so all must have different colours. **Three** colours work, however, on a cube – even though the cube has **more** regions. The trickiest case is the icosahedron, with twenty triangular regions.

Colouring of regular polyhedra

Deformation of the five solids as an exercise in rubber-sheet geometry creates their plane graphs which can be easily coloured

1 Tetrahedron
2 Cube
3 Octahedron
4 Dodecahedron
5 Icosahedron

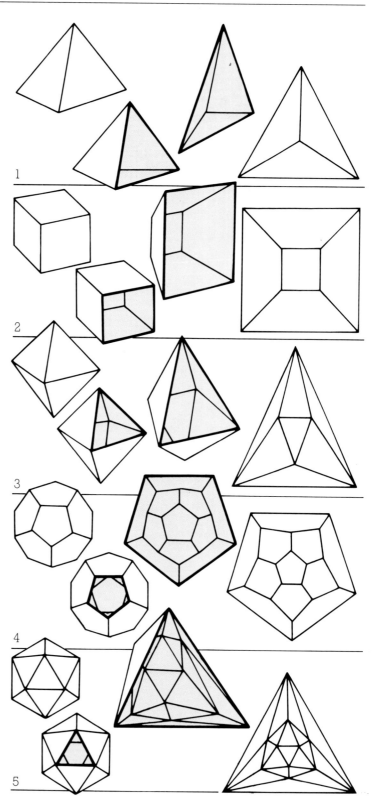

This is a delightful two-person game, based on the difficulty of seeing in advance the colour 'cul-de-sacs' that occur if you set about four-colouring a map. An apparently sensible choice of colours can lead to positions where no further colouring is possible.

Player A draws a region and colours it. Player B adds a new region, and colours that, according to the exact **opposite** of the domino principle.

Adjacent colours must **never** match. Play continues in turn until one player cannot move.

As a variation, a complicated map can be drawn before play starts; then players take turns to colour regions so that adjacent regions have different colours, until one player cannot move and loses. Only four colours are allowed in these games.

Colouring a map of 210 countries

Colour the map using four colours only

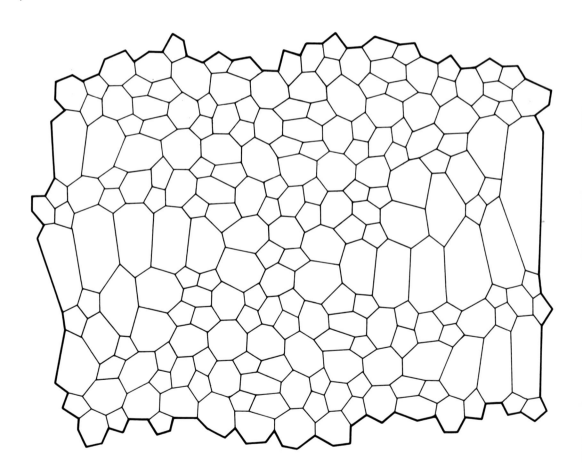

While four colours are needed for most maps, maps drawn in special ways may not need as many. An extreme case is where the maps are drawn using only straight lines. A little experiment suggests that **two** colours are then sufficient.
Is this true?
In fact it is, and the proof is quite easy. Add the lines one by one to the map. As each line is added, interchange the two colours on all regions that lie on **one side** of the new line. This makes the colours remain different across old boundaries; and also across the new one, thanks to the interchange of colours. The same proof can be generalized to apply to maps in which the boundaries are either single curves that run right across the whole plane, or closed loops.
All these two-colour maps have an **even** number of edges meeting at any junction. This must be true of any map that can be coloured with just two colours, because the regions around a junction or corner must be of alternate colours. More than this: it can be proved that any map on the plane can be coloured using only two colours if and only if all its junctions have an even number of edges meeting there. This is the **Two-Colour Theorem**.

The two-colour theorem

How many colours are needed for colouring these maps so that no two regions with a common border will have the same colour?

(Solution: page 123)

Brams' map-colouring game

In the simple map **n** is at least 5.
If no game is played according to the rules explained, the map can, of course, easily be coloured with four colours, as can any map on the plane

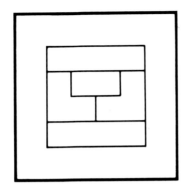

This is a more advanced map-colouring game, named after its inventor. Two players start with a given (but arbitrary) map, and a supply of **n** pencils of different colours. They take turns to colour the map one region at a time, so that no two adjacent regions have the same colour.
Player 1 is the **minimizer**. His aim is to play so that by the end of the game the entire map has been coloured with only **n** or fewer colours. If so, he wins.
Player 2 is the **maximizer**. He has to play with one of the **n** colours, **if that is possible**. If not, he wins.
The maximizer tries to play in such a way that, on some later move, the position becomes blocked. The minimizer, of course, tries to prevent this.
Even though the Four-Colour Theorem is true, this just means that there is some way to colour the map with four colours, assuming that the players cooperate. But this is a competitive game, so they don't, right?

Brams' map-colouring game – how to win the game

When five colours are used playing the map below, the maximizer can always win by following a simple strategy: to play always on the face of the distorted dodecahedron opposite the face where the opponent last played, using the same colour

(Solution: page 121)

There is an interesting theoretical question here. What is the smallest value of **n** (the number of colours) for which the minimizer can always win, no matter what map the game starts with? Brams has shown that some maps need **six** colours in this competitive version of the problem for the minimizer to win. That is, there exists a map such that with five colours the maximizer wins. The competitive game requires at least two colours more than the cooperative one. However, it is not proved that six is the answer. A larger number may be needed.

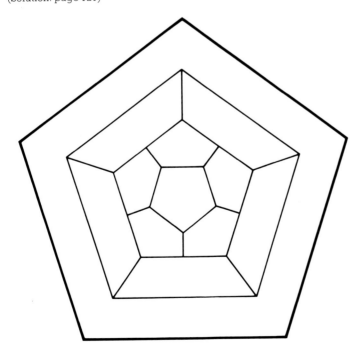

That is not the end of the map-colouring story. Another version allows different regions of the map to belong to the same 'empire', requiring the same colour on each part.

If each empire consists of exactly **m** regions, this is called the '**m**-pire' problem. The usual map-colouring problem is thus the 1-pire problem. For example, in the 2-pire problem, we consider all maps in which different regions are associated in pairs (into 2-pires, that is). The map must be coloured using the same colour on the two parts of each 2-pire, but of course different 2-pires can be different colours. (On old British maps, the British Empire was always red, the German Empire khaki. No doubt the Germans used a different colour scheme.) The analogue of the four-colour problem is now: how many colours suffice to colour all 2-pire maps? The answer is known, and it is twelve, surprisingly large. For 3-pires, it is eighteen.

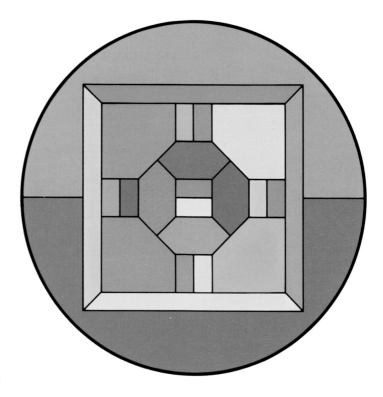

(above)
M-pire problem for **m** = 2

For a 2-pire map requiring twelve colours

(right)
M-pire problem for **m** = 3

For a 3-pire map requiring eighteen colours.
(Note that the third part of region 18 is disconnected on the plane)

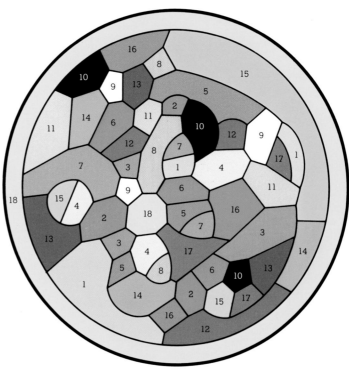

Another problem was proposed by Gerhard Ringel in 1950. Assume that the nations of the Earth have colonized Mars and that there is one region for each nation on each planet (the home country and its colony). Naturally, the countries will insist that Mars maps use the same colours for the colonies as Earth maps do for the home countries.

How many colours will suffice, in general?

This is like a 2-pire problem, but with the added restriction that the two parts of the 2-pire lie in two disjunct regions (Earth and Mars). So the number must be less than or equal to that for the 2-pire problem, which is twelve. Ringel showed it must be at least eight. So the answer is one of the numbers

$$8, 9, 10, 11, 12.$$

The question is which?

You should be able to think of other variations. Suppose everybody colonizes Venus? Suppose that instead of asking for all nations to have **m**-pires of the same **m**, we let them have **n**-pires where **n** is less than or equal to a fixed **m**? So different nations can have different numbers of regions.

What about the Earth–Mars problem when Mars is doughnut-shaped?

The Earth–Mars colouring problem

Colour the eleven 2-pires of the two spheres so that both regions having the same number are given the same colour.

What is the minimum number of colours needed?

(Solution: page 122)

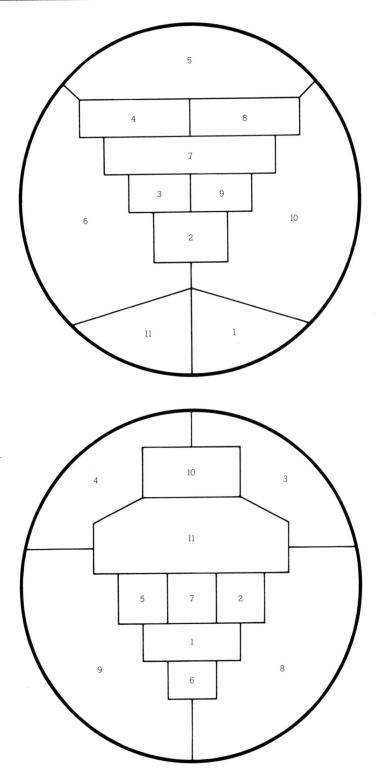

Mazes are ancient structures. Legend has it that the first maze was built by Daedalus to house the Minotaur, half bull, half monster, of King Minos of Crete. From this maze Theseus found his way back by using a ball of golden thread.

From the mathematical standpoint a maze is a problem in topology.

A maze can be solved quickly on paper by shading all the blind alleys until only the right route remains. But when you do not possess a map of the maze and you are inside it, the maze can be easily solved by placing your hand against the right (or left) wall and keeping it there all the time as you walk. You are sure to reach the exit, though your route may not be the shortest one.

This method does not work with mazes in which the goal is within the labyrinth and surrounded by closed circuits.

Mazes that contain no closed circuits are called 'simply connected', i.e. they have no detached walls. Mazes with detached walls are sure to contain closed circuits, and are called 'multiply connected'.

There is a mechanical procedure – an algorithm – which solves all mazes: as you walk through the maze, draw a line on one side of the path, say your right. When you come to a new juncture of paths, take any path you wish. If you later return to a previously visited juncture, turn around and go back the way you came.

If in walking along an old path (a path marked on your left) you come to a previously visited juncture, take any new path if one is available; otherwise take an old path. Never enter a path marked on both sides.

There are two fields of science in which interest in mazes remains high: psychology and the design of computers. Psychologists use mazes

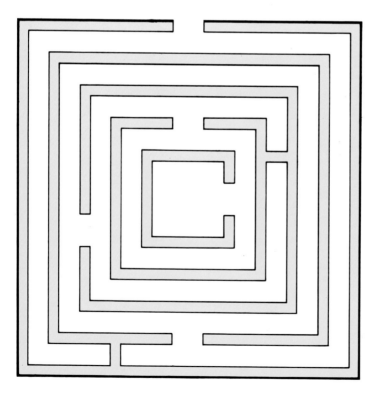

Mazes

Top: a simply connected maze

Bottom: a multiply connected maze

Maze problem

Follow a continuous path from door to door going through them all – never returning by the same way

(Solution: page 123)

to study the learning behaviour of animals. Even the earthworm can be taught to run a simple maze, but the rat is one of the favourite instruments for such investigations. Very early in these researches it was found that a rat could learn to find its way through highly complex mazes involving twenty or even more choices. Has the rat learned a sequence of movements (motor theory) or some kind of map (spatial-relationship theory)?

For computer designers, robot maze runners are part of an exciting programme to build machines which, like animals, profit from their experience. Many such machines – still toys – have already been built. They are the beginnings of future learning machines and robots which will play an enormously important role in the automatic machines of the space and electronic age.

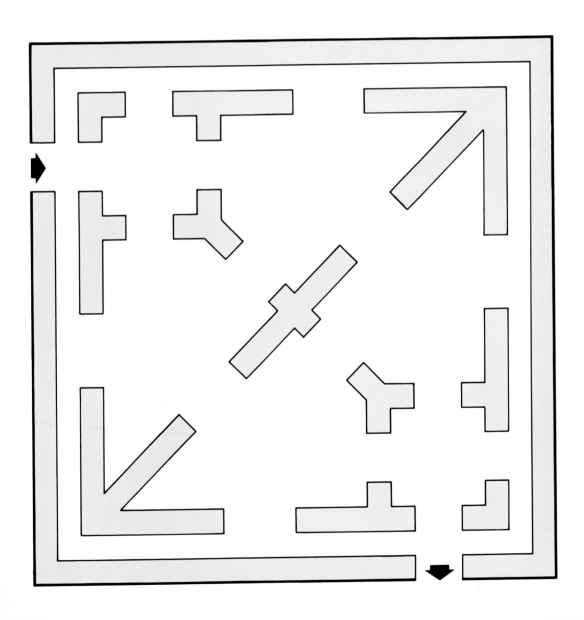

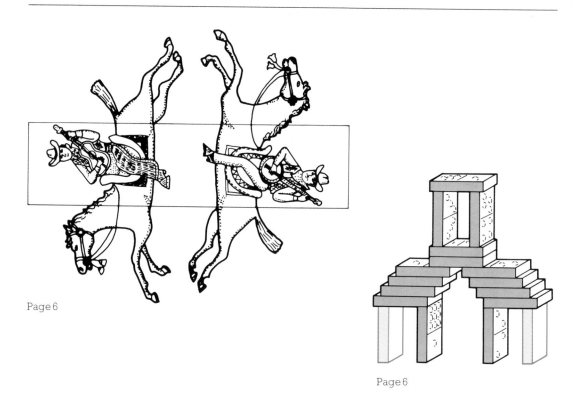

Page 6

Page 6

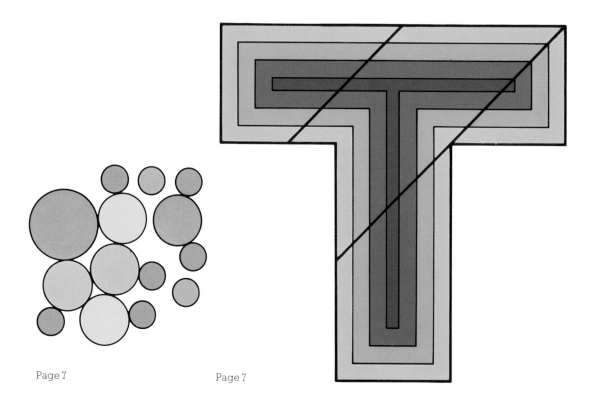

Page 7

Page 7

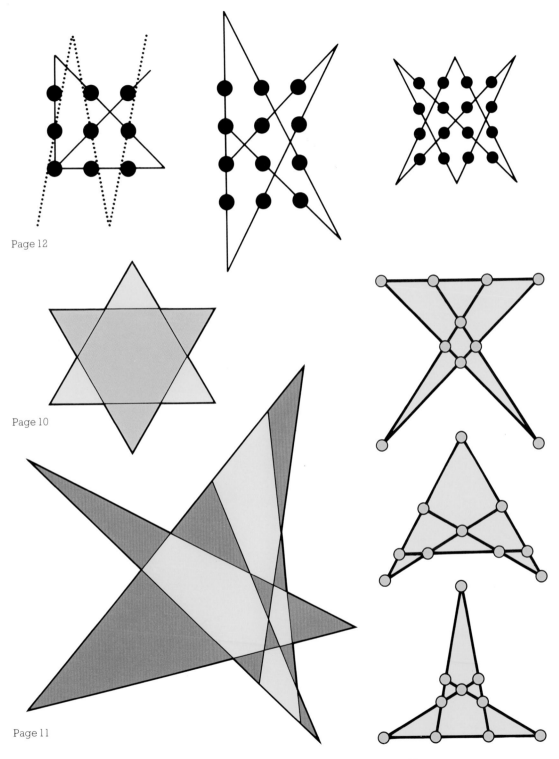

Page 12

Page 10

Page 11

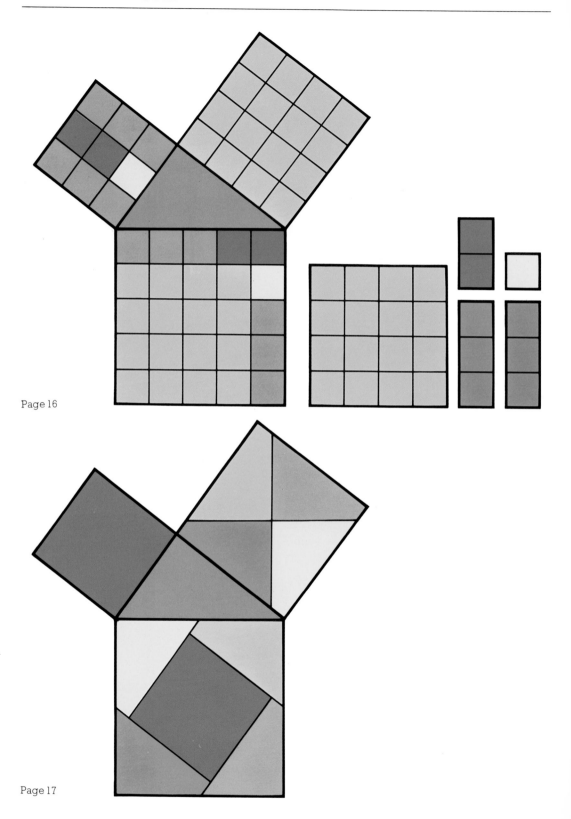

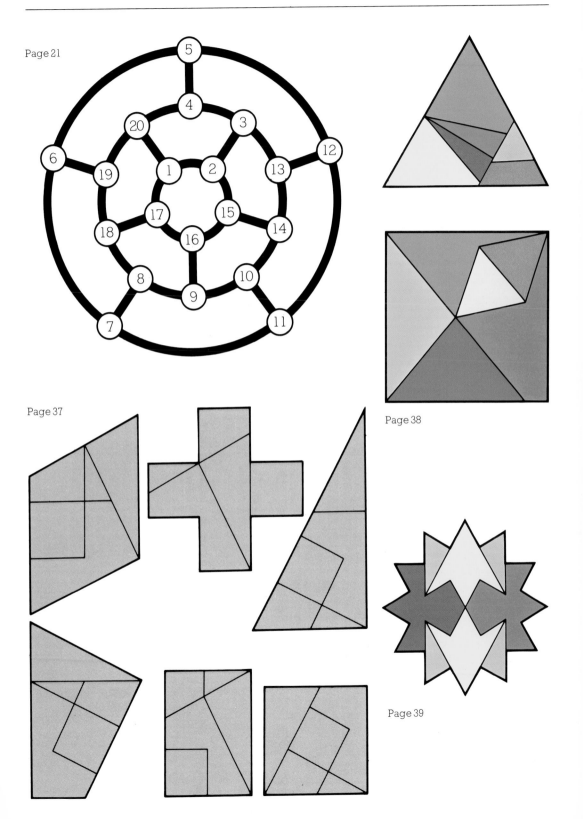

Page 21

Page 37

Page 38

Page 39

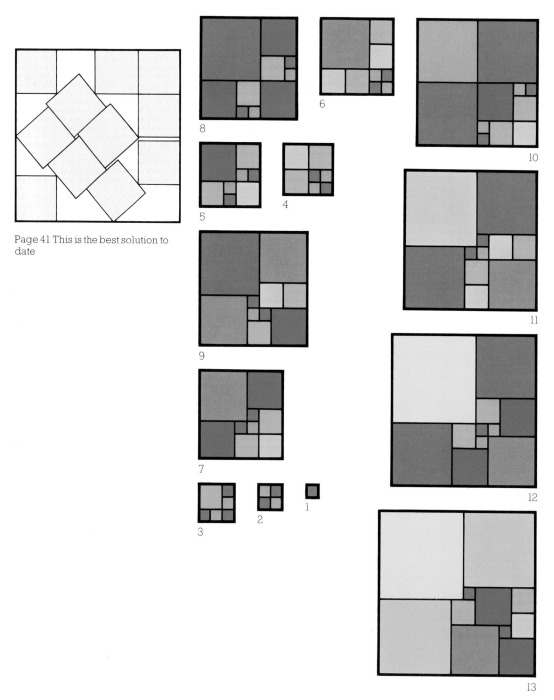

Page 41 This is the best solution to date

8

6

5

4

10

9

11

7

3

2

1

12

13

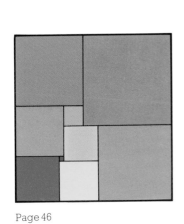

Page 46

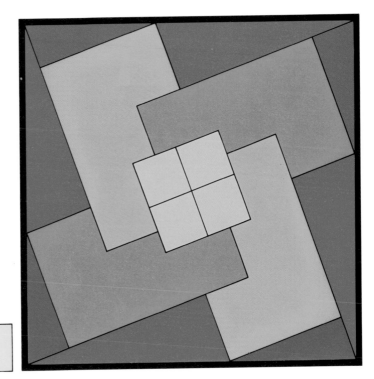

Page 47

Page 48

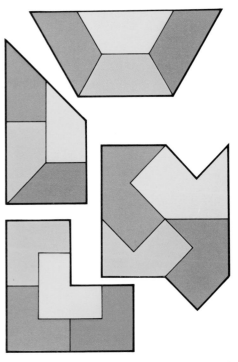

Page 49

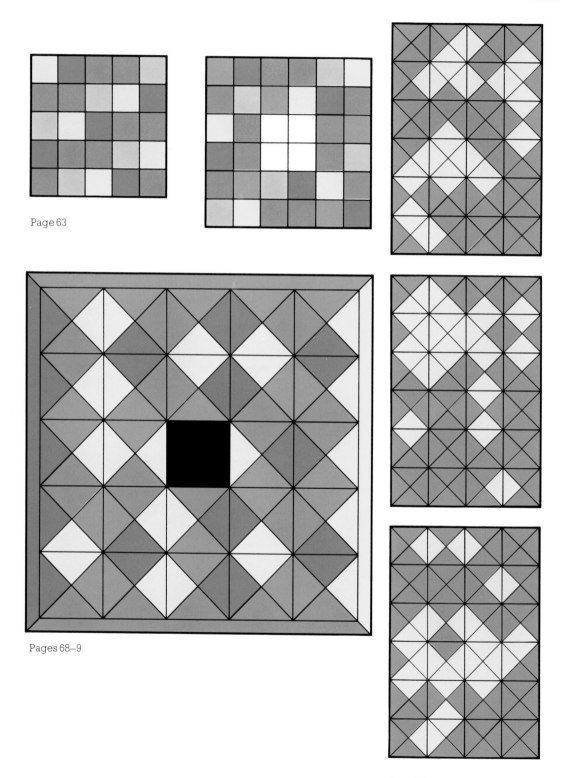

Page 63

Pages 68–9

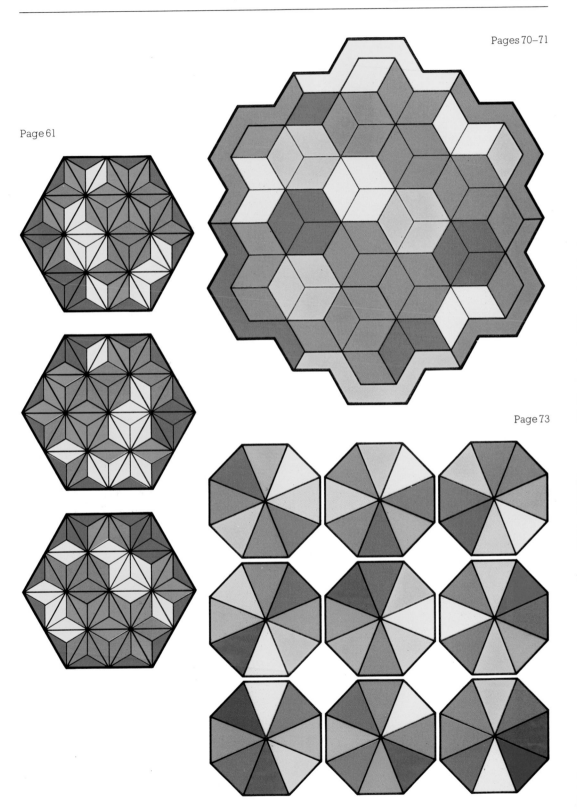

Pages 70–71

Page 61

Page 73

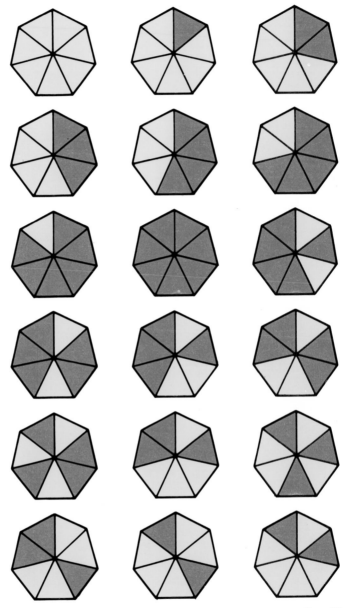

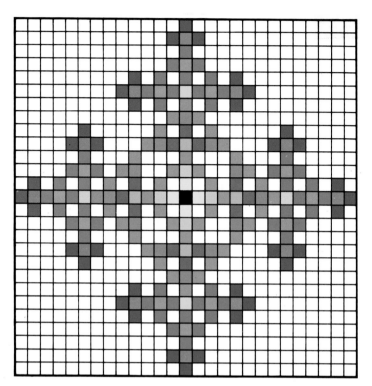

Page 88

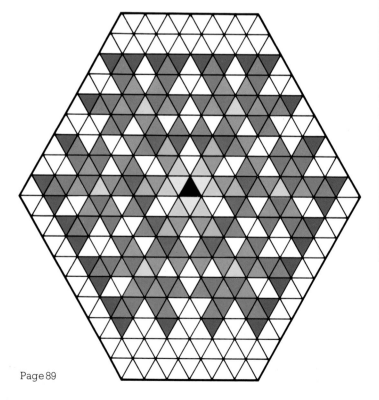

colour	□		△
1	4		3
2	4		6
3	12		6
4	4		6
5	12		12
6	12		18
7	36		12
8	4		6
9	12		12
10	12		24
11	36		30
12	12		24
13	36		30

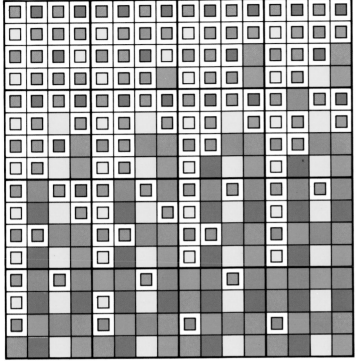

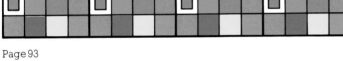

Page 93

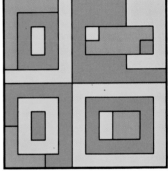

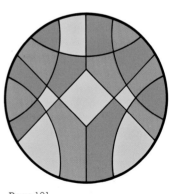

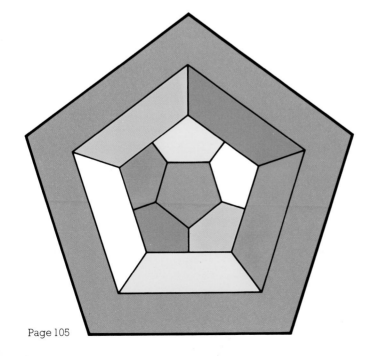

Page 101

Page 105

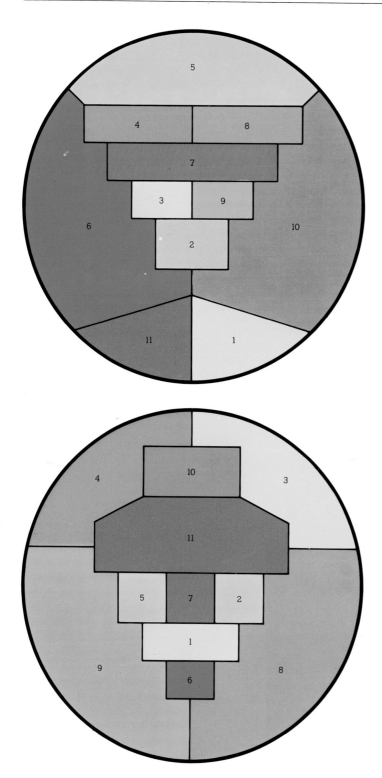

Page 104

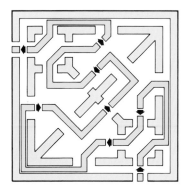

Page 109

124 References

Stephen Ainley, *Mathematical Puzzles*, G. Bell & Sons, 1977

W. W. Rouse Ball and H. S. M. Coxeter, *Mathematical Recreations and Essays*, University of Toronto Press, 1967

Stephen Barr, *Second Miscellany of Puzzles*, Macmillan, 1969

George C. Beakley and Ernest G. Chilton, *Design*, Macmillan, 1974

H. Martyn Cundy and A. P. Rollett, *Mathematical Models*, Clarendon Press, 1961

A. P. Domoriad, *Mathematical Games and Pastimes*, Pergamon, 1964

Martin Gardner, *Mathematical Circus*, Penguin Books, 1982

Martin Gardner, *Mathematical Magic Show*, Allen & Unwin, 1977

Harold R. Jacobs, *Mathematics and Human Endeavour*, W. H. Freeman, 1970

M. W. Keedy, R. E. Jameson, S. A. Smith and E. Mould, *Exploring Geometry*, Holt, Rinehart & Winston, 1967

David A. Klarner, *The Mathematical Gardner*, Wadsworth, 1981

Maurice Kraitchik, *Mathematical Recreations*, Dover, 1978

Frank Land, *The Language of Mathematics*, John Murray, 1962

Harry Langman, *Play Mathematics*, Hafner, 1962

Roger Millington, *Games and Puzzles for Addicts*, M. & J. Hobbs, 1979

Notes on Mathematics in Primary Schools, Cambridge University Press, 1961

Fred Schuh, *The Master Book of Mathematical Recreations*, Dover, 1968

D. E. Smith, *History of Mathematics* (2 vols.), Dover, 1951

H. Steinhaus, *Mathematical Snapshots*, Oxford University Press, 1969